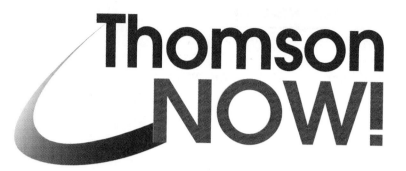

The Start Smart Guide
for instructors

AUSTRALIA ✦ BRAZIL ✦ CANADA ✦ MEXICO ✦ SINGAPORE ✦ SPAIN ✦ UNITED KINGDOM ✦ UNITED STATES

THE START SMART GUIDE FOR INSTRUCTORS

ACQUISITIONS EDITOR:
GARY WHALEN

DEVELOPMENT EDITOR: DEBORAH TODD

EDITORIAL ASSISTANT:
FIONA CHONG

TECHNOLOGY PROJECT MANAGER: TOM GREGA

MARKETING MANAGER:
TOM ZIOLKOWSKI

MARKETING ASSISTANT:
JENNIFER VELASQUEZ

MARKETING COMMUNICATIONS MANAGER:
NATHANIEL BERGSON-MICHELSON

PROJECT MANAGER, EDITORIAL PRODUCTION:
JENNIFER RISDEN

CREATIVE DIRECTOR: ROB HUGEL

PRINT BUYER: DOREEN SURUKI

COVER DESIGNER: FABIO FERNANDES

COVER PRINTER: QUEBECOR WORLD/TAUNTON

COMPOSITOR: LUNAR LOGIC DOCUMENTATION

PRINTER: QUEBECOR WORLD/TAUNTON

PRINTED IN THE UNITED STATES OF AMERICA
2 3 4 5 6 7 09 08 07 06

For more information about our
products, contact us at:
**Thomson Learning Academic
Resource Center
1-800-423-0563**

For permission to use material from
this text or product, submit a request
online at:
http://www.thomsonrights.com

Any additional questions about
permissions can be submitted by
e-mail to:
thomsonrights@thomson.com

**THOMSON HIGHER EDUCATION
10 DAVIS DRIVE
BELMONT, CA
94002-3098 USA**

ISBN 0-495-12604-7

ACKNOWLEDGEMENTS

WE ARE GRATEFUL TO THE FOLLOWING PEOPLE WHO REVIEWED NUMEROUS PROCESSES AND PROVIDED VALUABLE INSIGHT DURING THE DEVELOPMENT OF THE LATEST VERSION OF ThomsonNOW™.

ALISON AHLGREN
UNIVERSITY OF ILLINOIS

IRWIN J. BADIN
MONTCLAIR STATE UNIVERSITY

SUSAN CAIRE
DELGADO COMMUNITY COLLEGE

MARY ELIZABETH CAMP
INDIANA UNIVERSITY

CAROL D. CHENAULT
CALHOUN COMMUNITY COLLEGE

DENISE CUCURNY
CALIFORNIA STATE UNIVERSITY—LONG BEACH

JANICE L. EPSTEIN
TEXAS A&M UNIVERSITY

VERA HU-HYNEMAN
SUFFOLK COUNTY COMMUNITY COLLEGE

SINGH KELLY
UNIVERSITY OF WEST FLORIDA

FREDRIC KOLB
UNIVERSITY OF WISCONSIN—EAU CLAIRE

SCOTT MACDONALD
TACOMA COMMUNITY COLLEGE

MARILYN MASSEY
COLLIN COUNTY COMMUNITY COLLEGE

DAVID MAY
EASTERN WASHINGTON UNIVERSITY

MICHAEL MILLER
UNIVERSITY OF TEXAS AT ARLINGTON

SANJAY MISHRA
UNIVERSITY OF MEMPHIS

ALFONSO R. ODDO
NIAGARA UNIVERSITY

WESLEY A. PAYNE
DELGADO COMMUNITY COLLEGE

WENDIANN R. SETHI
SETON HALL UNIVERSITY

DAVID STRAAYER
WASHINGTON STATE UNIVERSITY

SVEN TRENHOLM
HERKIMER COUNTY COMMUNITY COLLEGE

ARUN VERMA
HAMPTON UNIVERSITY

CONTENTS

Contents

CREATING AND MANAGING ASSIGNMENTS. 57

GETTING STARTED

Welcome to ThomsonNOW, the integrated online learning system that gives you easy access to your courses, materials, and students when you need it most—at your pace, on your schedule. This Start Smart Guide is your how-to manual for getting started in ThomsonNOW. Use it as needed to get helpful information on setting up and managing your instructional needs.

Note: As a live, web-based program, ThomsonNOW is updated regularly with new features and improvements. Please refer to the ThomsonNOW online Help for the most current information.

The ThomsonNOW Plug-ins CD-ROM

ThomsonNOW requires a standard web browser, plus free "plug-in" software to run on your computer. The **Plug-ins** CD-ROM included with this guide provides browser software and several of the plug-ins you may need to run ThomsonNOW on your computer. While these programs are also available by free download from their suppliers, the CD offers a very convenient way to get set up all at once.

➤ To install the ThomsonNOW plug-ins software

1. Locate the ThomsonNOW **Plug-ins** CD-ROM included with this user guide.

2. Load the **Plug-ins** CD into your computer's CD-ROM drive.

3. Follow the on-screen instructions or browse to the appropriate folder to install the programs you need.

Note: You can also download individual programs from the ThomsonNOW Service Site at http://ilrn-support.com.

Registration and Sign-in

Instructors have three ways to get a ThomsonNOW Instructor account.
You can get one from your sales representative, or call 1-800-423-0563,
or request one online as follows:

1. Open a web browser and go to the ThomsonNOW Welcome page
   at http://www.ilrn.com.

2. Under **New Users**, click **Create an Account**.

3. On the **Registering** page, click **Instructor**.

4. Follow the on-screen instructions to submit your request.

Once your account has been set up with your e-mail address and
password, you will be able to sign in as a **Returning User** when you first
use ThomsonNOW.

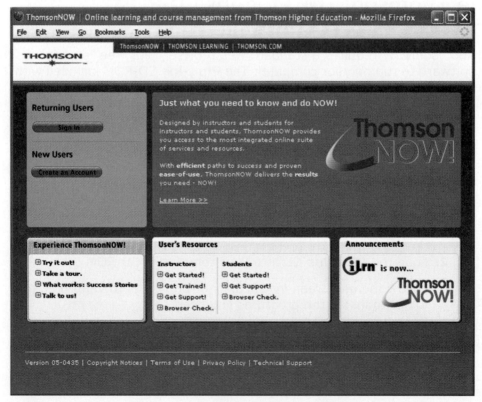

The ThomsonNOW Welcome page

Note: Students create their own accounts using **Content Access Codes** included with new textbooks (or purchased separately for used textbooks), or using **Course Keys** provided by their instructors. See "To generate a Course Key" on page 23.

Signing In as a Returning User

Once you have been assigned a ThomsonNOW account, you will sign in as a Returning User from anywhere you have Internet access.

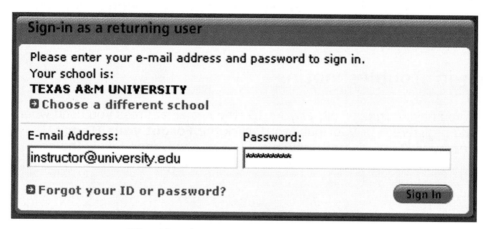

The Sign-in as a returning user box

➢ To Sign In to ThomsonNOW

1. Connect to the Internet and go to **http://www.ilrn.com**. The ThomsonNOW Welcome page opens.

2. Under **Returning Users**, click **Sign In**.

3. Check to see that the correct school name appears on the **Sign-in as a returning user** page. If you need to re-select your school name, click the **Choose a different school** link.

Note: Even if you have used ThomsonNOW before, the school name may be incorrect if you change computers or clear your browser "cookies."

---

4. Enter your e-mail address. Be sure to use the e-mail address you used when your account was created or you registered for ThomsonNOW.

5. Enter your ThomsonNOW password.

Note: If you need help remembering your ThomsonNOW e-mail or password, click the **Forgot your ID or Password?** link.

---

6. Click **Sign In**.

You will then see the System Check, which ensures you have the appropriate web browser and settings to run ThomsonNOW, and provides help messages if you need to change your settings. Once you complete the System Check, your **Home** page opens.

Sign-in Troubleshooting

If you have forgotten either your ID (the e-mail address you used when you registered) or your password, click the **Forgot your ID or Password?** link on the **Returning Users** page, then follow the on-screen instructions. For more detailed information, see the online Help.

THE HOME PAGE

After you sign in to ThomsonNOW, you will see your **Home** page. The **Home** page provides direct access to all the main "tabbed" areas of ThomsonNOW, such as **Assignments/Tests**, **Students**, and **Gradebook**. It also provides helpful tools and resources you will use often. Finally, you can use the **Home** page as a quick reference to your course status, as it contains tables with links to overdue assignments, current assignments, and recently graded assignments.

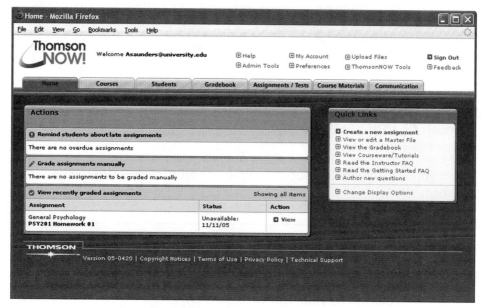

The ThomsonNOW Instructor Home page

Header Links

The top (the header) of every page in ThomsonNOW includes useful links for tools that you will use frequently as an instructor.

Help

Use this link to open the online ThomsonNOW Instructor Help at its main table of contents.

My Account

This link opens a page to edit your personal account information. You can access this page from the **My Account** link on your page header, or from the **Make changes to your account** link within **Admin Tools**.

Note: As a security measure, ThomsonNOW requires you to enter your current password before you can save any changes to your account.

You can edit any of the entries, and then save them by clicking the **Commit Changes** button at the bottom. The required fields are marked with a red asterisk (*) on-screen.

When you are done filling out the required fields, click **Save** to complete the form.

Note: You may get an error message if one or more of your entries does not match the required format. For example, phone numbers should include the area code, and use only hyphens (-) as separators. Follow the instructions of any error messages that appear to correct your entries, and then save your work.

Upload Files

Use this link to upload files into ThomsonNOW. You can upload copies of image, text, ZIP, or other files from your local computer onto the ThomsonNOW server for use in several areas of ThomsonNOW. For example, you can upload JPG graphics to insert in self-authored questions or to illustrate a course description.

Although you can upload almost any file type to the ThomsonNOW server, the ThomsonNOW editor can accept and display only browser-supported file types.

Note: The total number and size of files that you can upload depends on your ThomsonNOW user account "Upload Quota" setting. This setting can be changed by your ThomsonNOW System Administrator if you need more room.

➤ To upload a file onto the ThomsonNOW server

1. On your **Home** page header, click **Upload Files**. The **Upload files** page opens.

2. *(Optional)* In the **Uploaded Files** area, click the folder where you want to store the file.

3. In the **Choose Files to Upload** area, click **Browse**. Browse your way to the file you want to upload, select it, and then click **Open**. The file name appears under **Filename**.

   Note: If the file name includes spaces or special characters, they are removed.

   ---

4. *(Optional)* Choose additional files to upload by clicking **Browse**.

5. Click **Upload Queue** to upload and save the file or files to your area of the ThomsonNOW server. The file appears on the **Upload Files** page.

On the **Upload Files** page, you can also:

- Display the contents of files
- Rename and delete files
- Add descriptions of files
- Create folders to help you organize your uploaded files
- View the contents of a file in a separate browser window
- Download files so that you can copy them to another computer or view file types that do not display in the preview pane
- Copy, cut, and paste to copy or move files to different folders
- Unzip files

➤ To view the contents of a file in a separate browser window

1. Click the file name.

2. Click **View**.

Note: Use **Download** to view file types that do not display in a browser window or the preview pane.

➤ To delete a file from your ThomsonNOW server folder

1. Click the file name.

2. Click **Delete**.

Caution: Before deleting a file, be sure that it is not currently in use (referenced) in an existing course, assignment, or problem. Otherwise, deleting it will create a "broken link" and errors in your work. If you cannot verify that the file is not referenced, consider keeping it.

➤ To rename a file

1. Click the file name.

2. Click **Rename file**.

3. Enter the new name in the highlighted text box, and then click outside the box to save your changes.

Caution: Before changing a file name, be sure that it is not referenced from somewhere in ThomsonNOW. If you cannot verify that the file name is not referenced, consider uploading a duplicate version of the file with the new name instead.

➤ To add or edit a description

Descriptions are optional text you can use to remind you of the characteristics or usage of a particular file.

1. Click the file name.

2. Click **Change Description**.

3. Enter or edit the description, and then click **OK**. This description is visible only on the upload files pane.

➤ To create a new folder within the Your Files folder

1. Click **New Folder**.

2. Enter the folder name, and then click **OK**.

➤ To delete a folder

Select the folder, and then click **Delete**.

➤ To rename a folder

Select the folder, and then click **Rename**.

➤ To download a file from the ThomsonNOW server to your computer

1. Click the file name.

2. Click **Download**. Your browser's file-download window opens.

3. Click **Save**, browse to the location where you want to store the file, and then click **Save**.

➢ To unzip a file

Zip files let you store one or more files in one compressed package. You can upload files in ZIP format, and then unzip them on the server to work with the contents.

1. Upload the ZIP file into ThomsonNOW if you have not already.

2. Click the file name.

3. Click **Unzip**. The files are unzipped into the current folder.

➢ To copy files

1. Click one or more file names.

2. Click **Copy**. The files are copied to the clipboard.

➢ To cut files

1. Click one or more file names.

2. Click **Cut**. The files are copied to the clipboard. They are removed from their original folder only after you paste them into a new folder.

➢ To paste files

1. *(Optional)* Click the folder where you want to paste the files.

2. Click **Paste**. The files are moved from the clipboard to the folder. You cannot paste them again.

Sign Out

Use this link to sign out of the current ThomsonNOW session and return to the ThomsonNOW Welcome page.

Admin Tools

Use this link for tools that help you manage your ThomsonNOW accounts and books.

As a ThomsonNOW instructor, you can access the following functions from the **Admin Tools** link on the page header.

Bug reporter for testers

This area lets you create a preformatted bug report, which you can then forward to ThomsonNOW Technical Support as an e-mail.

Use the Bug Reporter to quickly prepare a ThomsonNOW bug report formatted with your system configuration and other relevant details. These preformatted fields contain information ThomsonNOW Technical Support may need when addressing your issue.

Make changes to your account

Use this page to update your personal ThomsonNOW account information. (You can also access this page directly from the **My Account** header link.)

Register for a new course

This page lets you register for your own course(s) as a student, or for courses created by another instructor.

View progress on assignments

Use this area to view your own progress as a student (if you have registered for a class as a student).

View your own assignments (as a student)

This area lets you view your own assignments as a student without going through the course registration process.

Preferences

The **Preferences** link, available from the page header, opens a window to let you control the general appearance of your ThomsonNOW pages and determine access to certain advanced features.

To view or change your current Preferences, sign in to ThomsonNOW and click the **Preferences** link at the top of the page. When you are finished making changes, click **Save these changes** to keep them, or **Cancel** to discard them.

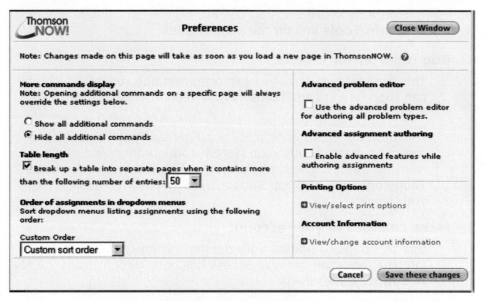

Instructor Preferences

More commands display

This setting lets you control the default appearance of all ThomsonNOW pages with **Show all commands/Hide these commands** links.

The Show/Hide links in ThomsonNOW keep additional or expert commands out of the way until you need them. If you use the expert commands a lot, you may wish to have your ThomsonNOW pages show them by default. You can always change this setting manually on any page.

To have all pages show all commands by default, select **Show all additional commands**.

To have all pages hide any additional or expert commands by default, select **Hide all additional commands**.

Table length

This setting lets you divide long tables or lists of information into specified "page lengths" of 20, 50, or 100 items. For example, you can use this setting to display a list of 100 students as one page of 100 students, two pages of 50 students each, or five pages of 20 students each. Whatever your preference, ThomsonNOW provides page controls to let you navigate between list pages easily. The default setting is 50 items.

To divide long lists of information, first select the check box **Break up a table into separate pages when it contains more than the following number of pages**. You can then select the page length from the following drop-down menu: 20, 50, or 100.

If you prefer not to have long lists divided into pages, clear the check box for **Break up a table into separate pages when it contains more than the following number of pages**.

Assignment sorting

This setting lets you select the default sorting method for assignment lists throughout ThomsonNOW, such as those in the **Assignments** tab and **Gradebook**. You can also reorder specific lists using the sort controls on that page. The default setting is "Custom Sort Order."

To select a default assignment list sort order, select the order type you want to use from the drop-down menu.

Advanced Problem Editor

This setting lets you use the Advanced Problem Editor exclusively for creating or editing self-authored questions of any problem type.

Currently, ThomsonNOW offers two authoring editors. The Standard Problem Editor provides a simplified default interface for creating basic problem types such as True/False. The Advanced Problem Editor has a more complex interface, but also provides more comprehensive functions and preview capabilities. Accordingly, some users prefer to use the Advanced Problem Editor even when working with the basic problem types normally presented in the Standard editor.

To use the Advanced Problem Editor only, select **Use the advanced problem editor for authoring all problem types**.

Advanced assignment authoring

This setting lets you access the Advanced Problem Editor so you can create or edit the more advanced self-authored questions and problem types.

ThomsonNOW features over 50 problem types you can use to create your self-authored questions. The 11 most commonly used problem types, including Multiple Choice, Fill in the Blank, and True/False, can be created using the default Standard Editor. To create the more complex or advanced problem types, however, you need to use the Advanced editor.

To access the Advanced Editor, select **Enable advanced features while authoring assignments**.

Note: To use only the Advanced editor for all problem types, select this option as well as the preceding option, **Use the advanced problem editor for authoring all problem types**.

Printing Options

Printing Options let you determine how your assignments and **Master Files** will be printed, and then save your settings. You can also access the Print Options from the **Assignments** and **Master Files** pages. See "Setting Print Options" on page 103 for details.

To access **Print Setup** from **Preferences**, click **View/Edit print options**.

Note: Some **Print Setup** options won't be available unless you already have a specific assignment selected.

Account Information

You can access the **Change Account** page to view or edit your current ThomsonNOW account profile, including your e-mail address, password, and contact information. You can also access this page from the main header **My Account** link.

To access Change Account from Preferences, click **View/Edit account information**.

ThomsonNOW Tools

Use this link to access several helpful utilities, calculators, a math/science glossary, and a wide range of interactive simulations.

Feedback

Click this link to open the **User Feedback Form**. Use the form to send ratings and comments to ThomsonNOW Technical Support.

Footer Links

The bottom (or footer) of every page in ThomsonNOW includes helpful information links, and the **Technical Support** link.

Technical Support

Click this link to open the **Contact Technical Support** form. Use the form to get help if you have a problem working with ThomsonNOW.

Quick Links

The **Home** page also includes a list of **Quick Links** for easy access to commonly used features, such as creating a new assignment or course, viewing your **Gradebook**, authoring new questions, changing your printing options, and changing your display options, among others.

Actions—The Assignments Table

Your Assignments table is labeled **Actions** and is the focal point of the **Home** page. It gives you quick access to taking action on assignments that need grading, sending reminders to students about late assignments, and viewing recently graded assignments.

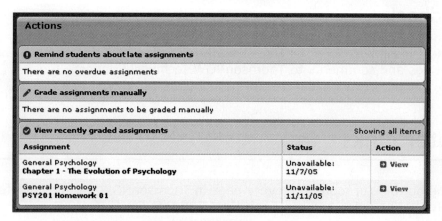

The Assignments table

Assignment Table Columns

Assignment

Click this link to view identification information on the course and assignment.

Status

View information on the due date, date modified, and date the assignment is no longer available.

Action

Click **View** to open the **Assignment Details** page. If you are viewing your assignments as a student, you can click **Take** to start the assignment.

COURSE MANAGEMENT

Courses provide the foundation for most of your instructor activities in ThomsonNOW. You can use the features on the **Courses** tab to create new courses and sections, manage course folders and permissions, and control course access. With one or more courses in place, you can then create assignments, enroll students, grade coursework, and manage the entire class using ThomsonNOW.

Setting Up Courses, Sections, and Folders

You will need to set up each course you want to manage in ThomsonNOW. At some schools, instructors set up their own courses. At others, the courses may be set up by an administrator or lead instructor. For instance, an instructor leading a discussion section of a larger course may not be the one setting up the main course in ThomsonNOW.

You can set up courses to contain multiple class sections, which is a common practice for large lecture classes with smaller discussion sections or labs. Each section is grouped under the course to which it belongs. This allows the course instructor to control assignment lists, grading, and other aspects of the course across all of its sections.

You can also use course folders to organize your courses and sections by class, department, term, or whatever works best for your school.

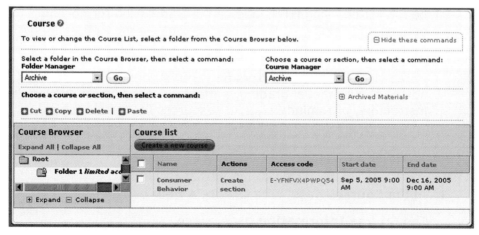

The Course page

Creating a Course

A course includes the following information:

Course Name

The name of the course as it appears in your department or institution catalog.

Course Number

The number of the course as it appears in your department or institution catalog.

Course Start date and End date

The start and end date of the course.

Note: These date entries are for your course description only. They have no effect on controlling enrollment, assignments, or grading.

You can enter the date directly, or click the **Calendar** icon to open the **Calendar Control** window.

Enrollment Limit

The maximum number of students who may enroll in your course.

The default setting is **No limit**, which allows any number of students to enroll.

Description

A text description of the course. You can copy and paste this text from your word processor, or enter it directly. A description can be formatted using HTML and can use advanced formatting options and links.

Notes

Notes viewable by instructors only, not students. For instance, advice about manual grading, a meeting schedule for section instructors, or reminders about resources for certain topics.

➤ To create a course

1. In the **Courses** page, click **Create a new course**.

   The **Course Information** page opens.

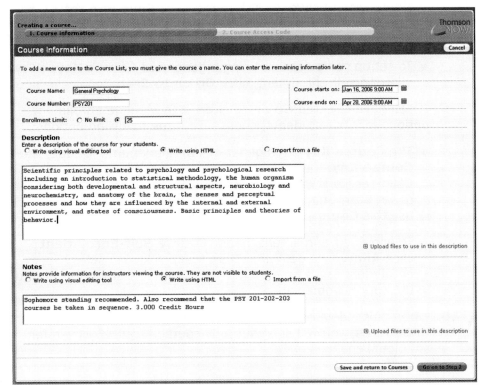

Creating a course

2. Enter the name of the course.

3. Enter the course number.

4. Click the Calendar icons to enter start and end dates.

5. If desired, enter the maximum number of students to be allowed to enroll.

6. Enter a course description to appear in the syllabus. You can copy and paste this text from your word processor, or enter it directly. You can then format the text using HTML and include hypertext links and ThomsonNOW equations.

7. Enter notes for yourself or other instructors.

8. You now have three options:

- If you wish to create sections, click **Save and return to Courses**. In **Courses**, you will see your new course listed with a **Create Course Section** link.

- If you wish to save your changes, click **Save and return to Courses**. In **Courses**, you will see your new course listed, available for additional changes.

- To set up course access using a generated **Course Key**, or by allowing self-enrollment, click **Go on to Step 2**.

9. If you have selected **Go on to Step 2** to manage enrollment options for your students, choose from the following options:

   - The **Course Key** page generates an alphanumeric code, the **Course Key**, that is unique for your specific class. Use the Calendar icons in the **Course Key Expiration Dates** section to set Start and End dates for the **Course Key**. Students will use this **Course Key** to register for your class.

   - To allow self-enrollment, under **Course Self-Enrollment** click **Allow** (the default is **Disallow**). Allowing self-enrollment saves time during setup, and lets students get into the course immediately.

10. When finished with Step 2, click **Save and return to Courses**. In **Courses**, you will see your new course listed, available for additional changes.

Creating Course Sections

Creating sections within a course provides separate **Gradebook** pages for each section, and allows for greater control of individual sections by instructors responsible for those sections.

A course can be divided into several sections. For example, you can set up a main lecture section, discussion sections, lab sections, and so forth. This feature also allows the main course instructor the ability to control aspects of the course assignments and grading across all course sections.

➤ **To create a course section**

1. With a main course created, click **Create Section** under **Actions**. The **Section Information** page opens.

2. Enter the name of the section.

3. Enter the course number for the section.

4. Click the Calendar icons to enter start and end dates.

5. If desired, enter the maximum number of students to be allowed to enroll in the section.

6. Enter a course description to appear in the syllabus. This description can be formatted text and can include hypertext links and ThomsonNOW equations.

Note: Use HTML formatting for the description and notes. You can choose to use the built-in HTML editor, import a text file, or copy and paste text from your word processor.

---

7. Enter notes for yourself or other instructors.

8. To save your changes, click **Save and return to Courses** *or*, to configure course access, click **Go on to Step 2**.

9. If you have selected **Go on to Step 2** to manage enrollment options for your students, choose from the following options:

- The **Course Key** page generates an alpha-numeric code, the **Course Key**, that is unique for your specific class. Use the Calendar icons in the **Course Key Expiration Dates** section to set Start and End dates for the **Course Key**. Students will use this **Course Key** to register for your class.

- To allow self-enrollment, under **Course Self-Enrollment** click **Allow** (the default is **Disallow**).

Course Key—Managing Enrollment

Once a course is created, you have several options for determining how students can enroll themselves in your class.

○ You can generate a **Course Key** and issue it to your students. ThomsonNOW automatically generates a code for your course when you click **Go on to Step 2** on the **Course Information** page.

○ To maintain strict control over enrollment, you can choose to enroll students manually on the **Students** tab. For details on manual enrollment, see "Managing Student Enrollment" on page 33.

○ Finally, you can allow self-enrollment, allowing any student at your school with ThomsonNOW access to sign up for the course.

Setting Up Student Enrollment

Course Keys provide the most convenient way to manage enrollment for your class or section. ThomsonNOW automatically generates a unique **Course Key** for each course. You can then provide the **Course Key** to your students via e-mail or printed syllabus to allow them to enroll themselves (or register for ThomsonNOW, if necessary).

Only students with the code will be able to enroll.

The **Course Key** page displays the current key for a course and provides options for managing the **Course Key**.

Generate a new code

You can generate a new **Course Key** if, for instance, you are planning on teaching a previous course in a new term. Old keys cannot be re-used.

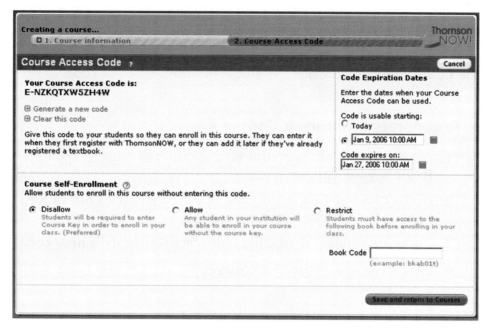

Generating a Course Key

➤ To generate a Course Key

1. Click the name of the course on the **Courses** page to open **Review your course**.

2. In the **Change** area to the right of the page, click **Course Key** to open the **Course Key** page.

3. On the **Course Key** page, under **Code Expiration Dates**, enter a starting date for this code to be valid, or accept **Today**.

4. Enter an expiration date for this code.

5. Click **Save and return to Courses**.

Change a Course Key

For each course you create, ThomsonNOW automatically generates a unique **Course Key**. You can change the **Course Key** for a course to account for changes in enrollment or class usage. For instance, at the beginning of a new term, you can copy a course and create and distribute a new **Course Key**. See "Copying, Deleting, and Moving Courses" on page 28.

Sometimes the **Course Key** that is automatically generated has a string of numbers or symbols that the instructor might not like, for example, a string with lowercase letter "l" and the number 1 in succession might look confusing to students. In such cases, you might want to regenerate the **Course Key** and provide the students with a different code.

➤ To generate a different Course Key

1. Click the name of the course on the **Courses** page to open the **Review your course** page.

2. In the **Change** area at the right of the page, click **Course Key** to open the **Course Key** page.

3. In the area under the existing code, click **Generate a new code**.

4. Click **Save and return to Courses**.

Clear this code

You can clear the key for a course. After you clear the **Course Key**, no additional students can register for the course and the key is no longer usable.

➤ To clear a Course Key

1. Click the name of the course on the **Courses** page to open **Review your course**.

2. In the **Change** area to the right of the page, click **Course Key** to open the **Course key** page.

3. In the area under the existing code, click **Clear this code**.

4. Click **Save and return to courses**.

Don't allow / Allow students to enroll right now

This option can prevent students from enrolling in a course.

> ## To prevent / allow student enrollment

1. Click the name of the course on the **Courses** page to open **Review your course**.

2. In the **Change** area at the right of the page, click **Course Key** to open the **Course Key** page.

3. Click **Disable Course Access Code**.

Note: This link changes to **Allow students to enroll**. Use that link to reverse the setting.

---

4. Click **Save and return to Courses**.

Course Self-Enrollment

This option allows any student at your school who is already registered for ThomsonNOW to enroll in the course without a **Course Key**. You can still provide a **Course Key** to help students register for ThomsonNOW, or have them register using the **Content Access Code** from their textbook.

Allow

Choose this option to allow any student with a local ThomsonNOW account to "self-enroll" in the course or section. If you allow self-enrollment, students will see a **Self-Enrollment** option on their **Home** page leading to a link for enrolling in the course.

Disallow

This option specifically disables the student auto-enrollment function. Students will need a **Course Key** to enroll, or will have to be enrolled manually via the **Students** page.

Note: Disallow is the default setting for self-enrollment.

Restrict

This advanced option lets students self-enroll only if they have satisfied the condition specified here. This option requires familiarity with ThomsonNOW formula coding logic.

Under this option, the **Book Code** box appears. You can use this box to confirm that the students have entered their **Content Access Code** for the course textbook. The syntax for this condition is **isBookVisible ("iLrnbookcode")**.

Note: You can see the ThomsonNOW book code(s) when you select books to draw items in **Create Assignment**. Examples: "exmp01g" or "tgie02s" or "ksac07t"

➢ To set course for self-enrollment

1. Click the name of the course on the **Courses** page to open the **Review your course** page.

2. In the **Change** area to the right, click **Course Key** to open the **Course Key** page.

3. Under **Course Self-Enrollment**, select **Allow**.

   You can also make this setting conditional. Use the **Make conditional** field to prevent students from registering for a course until specified criteria are met. The value you enter for this property is an expression that defines these limits for each student.

4. Click **Save and return to Courses**.

Code expiration dates

You can enter specific start and end dates and times for the code's use in a class. For instance, most universities have a fixed add/drop period for courses.

Save and return to Courses

Saves your changes.

Creating Folders

Creating folders is a simple and effective way to help keep your courses well organized. You can rename folders and change their file-sharing settings to suit your needs.

➤ To navigate the course folder tree

○ Open and close all of the folders on the course tree with the **+/-** icons.

○ Click on the folder icons to view the contents.

➤ To create a folder

1. On the **Courses** page, click **Show all commands**, if necessary, to display editing commands.

   Note: The ThomsonNOW interface remembers this show/hide setting. You can also control it globally from your **Home** page **Preferences** link.
   ---

2. In the **Course Browser**, click on the folder that will contain your new folder.

3. In the **Folder Manager** drop-down menu, select **Create a subfolder** and click **Go**.

   Your new folder appears inside the folder you selected. You can now change the folder-sharing setting, or rename the folder.

➤ To change folder-sharing setting

All new folders you create are designated as "private" by default, which means that only you can view or change the contents. You can allow ThomsonNOW to share your folders so that others can view the contents. Shared folders are marked with a small hand icon.

1. In the **Courses** page, in the **Course Browser**, select the folder.

2. In the **Folder Manager** drop-down menu, select **Make public or private** and click **Go**.

> **Note:** To access the course for editing, click on it from the **Selected Course** tree list or from the **Contents** area of the parent folder.

➤ To rename a folder

1. On the **Courses** page, in the **Course Browser**, select the folder.

2. In the **Folder Manager** drop-down menu, select **Rename** and click **Go**.

3. Enter a new name for the folder and click **Save**.

Modifying and Managing Courses

Over time, you may find it convenient to reuse most or all of an existing course. The **Courses** page clipboard functions make it easy to copy and update entire courses for a new term.

Copying, Deleting, and Moving Courses

Please remember these two key points when working with courses and folders:

○ Plan the organization of your folders in advance. Courses can be moved from one folder to another, but any enrollment information is lost. Do not move courses around during the term.

○ You can create folders in which to file your courses at any time. *To move courses, however, you must copy them into the new folder, rather than moving them.* Copying retains all syllabus information, but not enrollment information.

➢ To copy a course

1. Create a folder into which your course will be copied. See "Creating Folders" on page 27 for details.

2. On the **Courses** page, in the **Course** list, select the box next to the course to be copied.

3. In the **Clipboard** area, click **Copy**.

4. Use the **Course Browser** to navigate to the destination folder.

5. Click **Paste from clipboard**.

The course information has now been copied into your new folder. By selecting the folder, you will find you now have the course information, name, syllabus, and assignments available for use in a new school term.

➢ To delete a course

1. On the **Courses** page, in the **Course** list, select the box next to the course to be deleted.

You can select more than one course at once.

2. In the **Clipboard** area, click **Delete**.

3. Click **OK** to verify permanent deletion of the course.

➢ To move a course

1. On the **Courses** page, in the **Course** list, select the box next to the course to be moved.

2. In the **Clipboard** area, click **Cut**.

3. Use the **Course Browser** to navigate to the destination folder.

4. Click **Paste from clipboard**.

Archiving Courses

Archiving courses works much the same way as archiving assignments. Select the course you want to archive on the **Course List**, choose **Archive** from the **Course Manager** drop-down menu, and click **Go**. For details on archiving your courses, folders, and assignments, see "Working with Archived Materials" on page 113.

Review Your Course Information

The **Courses** page provides you with the ability to quickly check information about your courses by clicking the respective course **Name** on the **Course list**. The **Review your course** page opens.

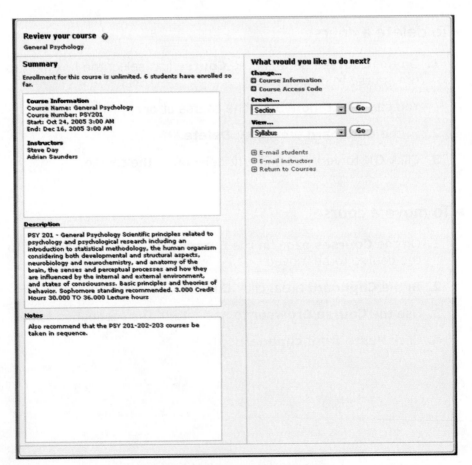

The Review your course page

The left side of the **Review your course** page gives you a brief enrollment **Summary**, and **Course Information** that includes the course name, number, instructor's name, and start and end dates, as well as the course **Description** and **Notes** (if any). On the right side, under **What would you like to do next?**, you have these options:

Change

- **Course Information.** This lets you edit the Course Information, such as name, start and end dates, description, and notes.

- **Course Key.** This link returns you to the **Course Key** page where a new **Course Key** can be generated, the start and expiration dates can be changed, and self-enrollment can be allowed or disallowed.

Create...

- **Section**. Select **Section** from this drop-down menu and click **Go** to create a section for this course. See "Creating Course Sections" on page 20 for more information.

- **Assignment**. Select **Assignment** from this drop-down menu and click **Go** to create a new assignment for this course. See "Creating New Assignments" on page 58 for more information.

- **Student account**. Select **Student account** from this drop-down menu and click **Go** to go to the **Students** page. See "Managing Student Enrollment" on page 33 for more information.

View...

- **Syllabus**. Select **Syllabus** from this drop-down menu and click **Go** to view the **Syllabus** page for this course.

- **Students**. Select **Students** from this drop-down menu and click **Go** to view the **Students** page for this course.

- **Assignments**. Select **Assignments** from this drop-down menu and click **Go** to view the **Assignments** page for this course.

- **Grades**. Select **Grades** from this drop-down menu and click **Go** to view the **Gradebook** page for this course.

E-mail students

Click this link to e-mail one or more students in your course or section.

E-mail instructors

Click this link to e-mail all instructors for the course or section.

Return to Courses

Click this link to return to the **Courses** page.

Date/Time Formatting

For most fields in which you need to enter a date or time (e.g., **Due Date**) you will have the **Calendar Control** tool available. If you prefer to type in dates and times directly, or are working with a field that does not provide the **Calender** tool, please follow these guidelines.

Date formatting guidelines

- ○ April 5, 1999, 2pm
- ○ 4/5/99 14:00
- ○ 4-5-1999 3:16am
- ○ 4 5 99
- ○ April 5 99
- ○ Thu May 31 2001 1:55P
- ○ 2001 May 31 16:45:00
- ○ For month, use the full name, or these abbreviations: Jan, Feb, Mar, Apr, May, Jun, Jul, Aug, Sep, Oct, Nov, Dec.

Time formatting guidelines

- ○ HH:MM (i.e., 1:20)
- ○ (number)(unit), where unit is s (second), m (minute), h (hour), d (day). Examples: 10s = 10 seconds; 10m = 10 minutes; 10h = 10 hours; 10d = 10 days; .5h = 30 minutes.

MANAGING STUDENT ENROLLMENT

As an instructor, you can use the features on the ThomsonNOW **Students** tab to manually enroll and withdraw students and instructors in your courses and sections. For example, you might want to manually add a student who comes to your office requesting to add the course. Or you might want to maintain rigorous control over course enrollment for an advanced seminar.

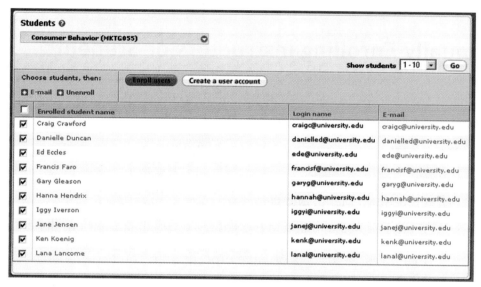

The Students page

There are several ways to enroll students in your courses and sections. Many instructors simply use the **Course Key** code that is automatically generated when the course is created. By posting this **Course Key** in the in-class materials or e-mailing it to students, the instructor lets students enroll themselves. For details on working with **Course Keys** and other self-enrollment options, see "Course Key—Managing Enrollment" on page 22.

Student enrollment is sometimes managed by a ThomsonNOW administrator or a lead teacher. If you have the appropriate account permissions, you can create student accounts and enroll those students directly.

You must also use the enrollment functions if you are creating a course with sections you want to assign to other instructors, such as teaching assistants. To assign the sections, you enroll those instructors as instructors in their sections of the course.

Note: To enroll instructors, you must first make sure that their ThomsonNOW accounts have been created. Instructor accounts can be created only by users with Administrator access. See "Registration and Sign-in" on page 2.

Manually Enrolling Instructors or Students

Follow these steps to add specific students or instructors to a course:

➢ To enroll instructors or students in a course

1. Click the **Students** tab, select the course or section from the drop-down menu, and click **Go**.

   If anyone has enrolled in the course or section, their enrollment information will appear in list form. For a long list, use the **Previous**/**Next** links or page drop-down menu to see more students.

2. Click **Enroll Users**. You will see the list of registered ThomsonNOW users eligible to enroll for the course or section in the lower left-hand area of the page.

3. In the upper right-hand area of this page, select **Enroll Students** or **Enroll Instructors**. The list of eligible users will appear.

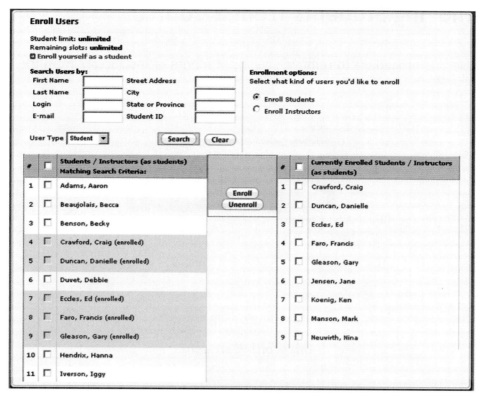

The Enroll Users page

4. To find a particular person, or to limit the list, use the provided search filters by entering the appropriate information in the boxes in the upper left-hand area of the page. You can search by first name, last name, sign-in ID, e-mail address, street address, city, state, or student ID number.

5. When you see the instructor(s) or student(s) you want to enroll, select the check boxes next to their name(s) and then click the **Enroll** button. The names will appear in a list in the lower right-hand area.

If you'd like to **Enroll yourself as a student** in your course, you can do so with the link in the upper right area of the page.

Note: To unenroll users, select the check boxes next to their names in the lower right-hand area, and then click the **Unenroll** arrow icon. The names will now appear in the list in the lower left-hand area. You can also unenroll students in the enrollment list view by selecting the check boxes next to their name(s), then clicking **Unenroll** in the toolbar.

Removing Students from a Course

Use this procedure to remove specific students or instructors from the course.

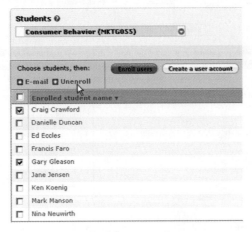

Unenrolling students

➢ To remove students from a course

1. From the **Students** page, select the course or section from the drop-down menu and click **Go**.

2. Select the check box next to a student's name (you can select multiple students), and then click **Unenroll**.

Your selected student is now unenrolled from your course or section.

Creating a Student Account

If you need to add a new student account for one of your students, follow these steps. You can also edit student accounts.

Note: Depending on how your school uses ThomsonNOW, creating student accounts may be restricted to ThomsonNOW administrators, or require you to have additional ThomsonNOW account privileges.

➤ To create a student account

1. From the **Students** page, select the course or section from the drop-down menu. Click **Go**.

2. On the main **Students** enrollment list, click **Create a user account**. The **Create a User Account** page opens.

3. Enter the student's information in the appropriate boxes, then click **Add user**. A message will appear, notifying you that the student has been successfully created.

4. To enroll the student you've just created in the course, simply click **Enroll Student** at the bottom of the page.

The student's name will now appear in your course section list.

➤ To edit a student account

1. From the **Students** page, select the course or section from the drop-down menu, and click **Go**.

2. Check the box next to the student name and click **Edit a user account**. The **Edit Record** page opens.

3. Change the appropriate information on the user account page. When the information is correct, click **Save**.

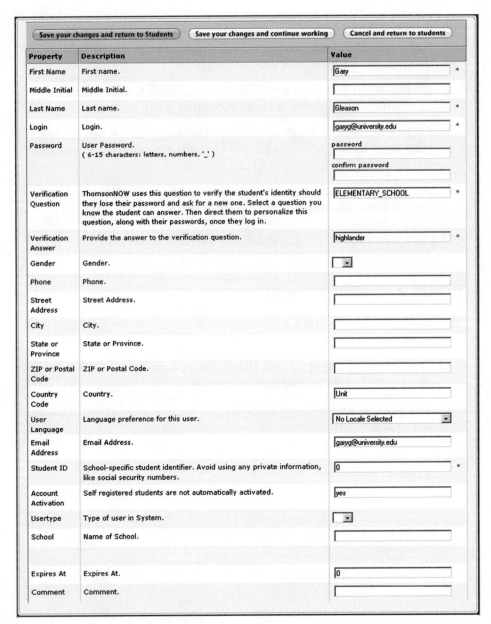

Property	Description	Value
First Name	First name.	Gary *
Middle Initial	Middle Initial.	
Last Name	Last name.	Gleason *
Login	Login.	garyg@university.edu *
Password	User Password. (6-15 characters: letters, numbers, '_')	password confirm password
Verification Question	ThomsonNOW uses this question to verify the student's identity should they lose their password and ask for a new one. Select a question you know the student can answer. Then direct them to personalize this question, along with their passwords, once they log in.	ELEMENTARY_SCHOOL *
Verification Answer	Provide the answer to the verification question.	highlander *
Gender	Gender.	[▾]
Phone	Phone.	
Street Address	Street Address.	
City	City.	
State or Province	State or Province.	
ZIP or Postal Code	ZIP or Postal Code.	
Country Code	Country.	Unit
User Language	Language preference for this user.	No Locale Selected [▾]
Email Address	Email Address.	garyg@university.edu
Student ID	School-specific student identifier. Avoid using any private information, like social security numbers.	0 *
Account Activation	Self registered students are not automatically activated.	yes
Usertype	Type of user in System.	[▾]
School	Name of School.	
Expires At	Expires At.	0
Comment	Comment.	

Save your changes and return to Students **Save your changes and continue working** **Cancel and return to students**

The Edit Record page

GRADEBOOK

ThomsonNOW automatically grades everything it can electronically, marks items that must be manually graded, and calculates a student's final grade or "grade to date."

Once the student finishes the assignment, you can use tools found in the **Gradebook** to review the answers, score any items requiring manual grading, and, if necessary, adjust scoring for any item, student, or assignment.

Some problem types require manual grading, such as Essay, Pencil Sketch, GraphSketch, Sketch2D, or combination problems that have these problem types as components. For assignments containing combination problems, ThomsonNOW will grade the electronically gradable parts, flag the manually graded items for your subsequent review and grading, and then calculate the student's grade to date.

ThomsonNOW also offers a wide range of grade-reporting options to help you summarize and analyze individual and class performance. You can review these reports online or print them out in a variety of formats.

Gradebook Terminology

There are many ways to customize and weight assignment and course grading. Familiarize yourself with the **Gradebook** terms to understand how the course grade is calculated.

Total Score

Total score is the sum of each assignment's score multiplied by the assignment's weight. Most problems have a default score of 1.0 for a correct answer, so the assignment score simply totals the number of correct answers. However, ThomsonNOW offers many ways to set up and score problems to adjust or weight this value.

- The problem can be authored to allow partial credit for some responses.

- You can adjust each problem's possible score on the assignments tab. See "Creating New Assignments" on page 58 for details.

- You can alter the possible score of the entire assignment with the **Possible Score** and **Grade on a Curve** assignment options. See "Creating New Assignments" on page 58 for details.

- You can adjust the scores of whole groups of assignments by putting them in assignment categories and weighting the category.

Note: Only assignments that are past due or have already been taken are included in the total score. Any points from extra-credit assignments are then added to the total.

Possible Score

This is the number of points a student could earn if he or she achieved a perfect score.

Extra Credit

Assignments can be set up as extra credit in the assignment options. Points earned as extra credit are added to the points earned, but not to the total points possible, when calculating the total percent grade (Total Score/Possible Score = Overall Grade). For example, suppose you set up a class with nine regular assignments and one extra-credit assignment. If each assignment is worth 10 points, the possible score for the course is 90. But a student who scored 100% on everything, including the extra-credit assignment, would get 100/90 = 111% for the course.

Category Score

Category Score represents a student's grade for each category of assignments in the course. Categories are optional—you create them on the **Gradebook** page as a means to adjust score weighting for a whole group of similar assignments. If you have not created any categories beyond the initial default category, the default category score is the final score for the course. See "Creating and Editing Assignment Categories" on page 42.

Category score is calculated as follows:

Category Score = (Total Score/Possible Score) x Category Weight (if any).

The category weight is a value that you set. Only categories containing at least one assignment that has been taken or is past due are counted.

Final Score

The final score is the sum of the category scores and reflects the student's grade for the course. If a category is empty (i.e., the assignments have not yet been taken), that category's score is excluded.

The Gradebook Page

The **Gradebook** page displays the names of all students enrolled in a course and their individual scores for assignments.

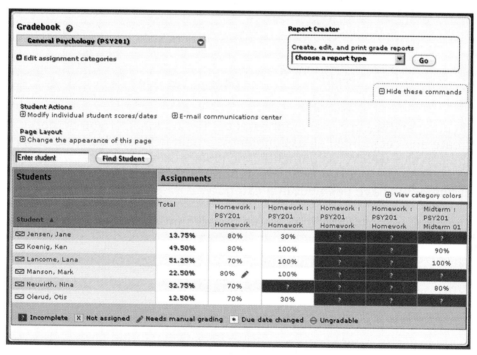

The Gradebook page

Note: You can change the way student, assignment, and grade information is presented on the page.

Creating and Editing Assignment Categories

Assignment categories let you group assignments by type so they can be weighted collectively in final grade calculations done automatically by ThomsonNOW. For example, you can create a category containing homework assignments and weight it to 30 percent of the course grade. This weighting will apply whether the category has 5 homework assignments or 50. Once you create an assignment category, you can add individual assignments to it here, or by using the assignment's **Category** option.

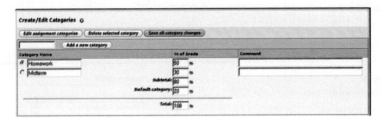

The Create/Edit Categories page

Creating and using assignment categories is optional. If you do not create any categories, all assignments remain in the default category. You can also weight assignments individually using the **Possible score** and **Grade on a curve** assignment options, regardless of whether the assignments have been put in a category.

The category weighting is applied after accounting for the weighting of individual assignments.

➤ To create assignment categories

1. Go to the **Gradebook** page.

2. Select a course or section in the drop-down menu and click **Go**.

3. Click **Edit assignment categories**. The **Create/Edit Categories** page opens.

4. Enter a name.

5. Click **Add a new category** and add the category you want (for example, Homework, Text, or Final Exam).

6. A name appears, and a place to enter a percentage appears. Enter a percentage.

7. In the input field to the left of **Add a new category**, delete the category that's there and type in a new one.

8. Click **Add a new category**. That category will appear below. Enter a percentage, and continue to add categories until finished.

9. Check that the percentages all add up to 100% of your newly created categories.

10. Save the category changes.

Note: You can also put a Comment by your category; for example, for a Homework category, you can add the comment "due weekly."

> ## To edit assignment categories

1. Go to the **Gradebook** page.

2. Select a course or section in the drop-down menu and click **Go**.

3. Click **Create/Edit assignment categories**. The **Create/Edit Categories** page opens.

4. To delete a category, click the button next to the category you wish to delete, and then click **Delete selected category**.

5. For existing assignments, to change a category or place a created assignment in a category, click **Edit assignment categories**.

6. Under the **Category** column, use the drop-down menu to select the appropriate category for each assignment. Click **Save all category changes**.

7. If you need to change available categories or add categories, click **Edit categories for this course**, and you will be returned to the **Create/Edit Categories** page.

8. Do one of the following:

   • Select an assignment from the **Assignments** drop-down menu, and click **Edit Grades**.

   • Click on the assignment date at the top of the column. (Moving your mouse over the assignment date will display the assignment name above the date headers.)

9. Click **Change Category** just under the **Find** button. The **Assign Categories** page opens.

10. Click **Edit categories for this course**.

Edit Grade Details

The **Edit Grade Details** page allows you to view and edit scores for individual problems and enter comments for student viewing. The lower half of the page contains a table of the problems in the assignment.

Below the table of problems is an e-mail link to technical support. Use this to report any grading errors you may have discovered.

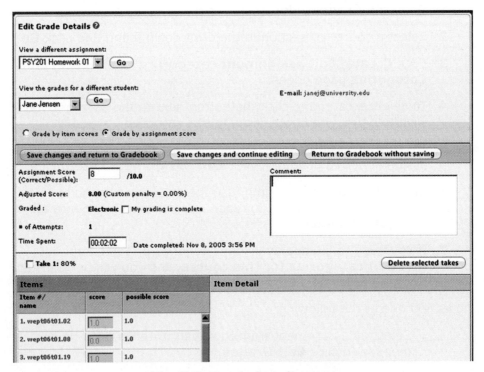

The Edit Grade Details page

Using the Edit Grade Details Page

You can view/edit grades for a single student on a single assignment. From the **Gradebook** page, click on the score you want to examine. This takes you to the **Edit Grade Details** page.

The **Edit Grade Details** page allows you to edit the following items:

Assignment Score

Adjust the student's overall assignment score by entering the number of correct answers in the **Assignment score** input box. (This yields the same result as changing it on the **Edit Assignment Details** page). Any **Late Penalty** previously assigned will still apply. When you save the grade change, the score will be marked (on the **Assignment Details** page) as "manually graded."

Graded

Any time you view an assignment on this page and click **Save your changes and return to Gradebook**, the **My evaluation** column on the **Assignment Details** page shows the assignment as "Evaluated," along with the date.

When you manually change a grade and save your changes, that item is marked as "Graded."

To mark an item as "Graded" that you have not manually adjusted, check **Fully Graded**, and **Save** your changes.

Note: At any point in your work, you can click **Save changes and continue editing**, **Save changes and return to Gradebook**, or **Return to Gradebook without saving**.

Comment

Enter a short comment to the student regarding this assignment or the grading. The comment will be visible in the **Notes** column of the **Student Details** page and on the student's **Progress** page.

Delete Selected Take

When a student has taken an assignment one or more times, it is possible for an instructor to delete a specific take. The takes are displayed, with sequential numbers and results in the lower half of the page.

Click on any take to select it, and click **Delete selected takes**.

To stay in this view for *another student,* select the student's name in the drop-down menu under **View the grades for a different student**, and click **Go**.

Note: You can also e-mail the student from this page by clicking the student's name next to **E-mail:** on the upper right side of the page.

To edit grading options for a *different assignment* for the current student, use the drop-down menu under **View a different assignment** at the upper left side of the page. Click **Go**.

Once finished, click

- ○ **Save changes and return to Gradebook**, or

- ○ **Save changes and continue editing** (your changes will be saved, and you'll remain on this page), or

- ○ **Return to Gradebook without saving**, and anything you entered will not be saved and it will return to its original state.

Editing Problem Scores

The lower half of the **Edit Grade Details** page allows you to edit the results of individual problems.

➤ To edit individual problem scores

1. On the **Edit Grade Details** page, click on a problem name.

   The screen refreshes, displaying the problem name, a score input box, a comment input box, and the text of the question. Beneath this is the student's score, student's answer, and the correct answer (if different from the answer given by the student).

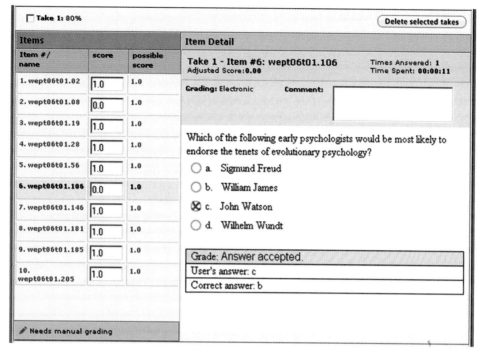

Editing problem scores

2. Enter a new score in the score input box.

3. Enter any comment you wish to make.

Caution: If you enter a comment for the problem and want the student to be able to see it, the assignment must be set up so the student can view grade details. See "Creating and Managing Assignments" on page 57.

---

4. To save your changes, click **Save changes and return to Gradebook** or **Save changes and continue editing**.

○ Use **Previous** and **Next** to navigate through the list of problems, or click a problem name.

○ Click the **x** next to the navigation links to close the problem view.

Grades by Student

From the **Gradebook**, click on the student name to go to the **Student Grade Details** page. This page displays all assignment grades for an individual student.

Links from this page allow you to edit student grades. The view is similar to the student's **Progress** page.

Assigned work appears first, with assignment scores, times taken, time spent, and any notes you may have entered, followed by non-assigned work.

Note: To switch to the **Assignment Grade Details** page (that is, a single assignment for students), click on the assignment name.

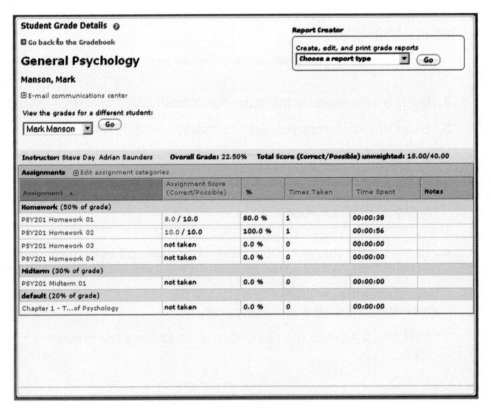

Student Grade Details page

The following tools are available to you on the **Student Grade Details** page:

E-mail communications center

Click this link to access your e-mail and send an e-mail to the selected student.

View the grades for a different student

Select a name from this drop-down menu, which contains all students enrolled in the displayed course, and click **Go**.

Report Creator

Select a report type from the drop-down menu, and click **Go**. The **Report Creator** opens in a new window. For more information, see "Grade Reports" on page 52.

Edit assignment categories

To edit current categories and create new categories, click this link at the top of the assignment list. For more information, see "Creating and Editing Assignment Categories" on page 42.

Sort the assignment list

Click any column header to sort the entire assignment list based on the information in that column. Click it again to reverse the order. The default display is sorted by assignment type.

Return to the **Gradebook** page by clicking **Go back to Gradebook**.

Grades by Assignment

Here you can see all student scores for a single assignment.

To get to the **Assignment Details** page:

1. On the **Gradebook** page, select a course or section in the drop-down menu and click **Go**.

2. Click on the assignment name at the top of the column. (The assignment name will be displayed above the scores for that assignment.)

Note: To change to the **Student Grade Details** page, click on the student's name.

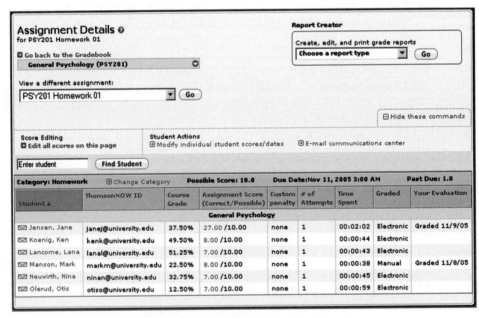

The Assignment Details page

Basic Options

Report Creator

Access basic reports by selecting them from the drop-down menu and clicking **Go**. See "Grade Reports" on page 52.

View a different assignment

Use the drop-down menu to choose a different assignment to view, and click **Go**.

Find Student

To search for a specific student's information, enter the student's name, and click **Find**.

Change Category

Click **Change Category** to go to the **Assign Categories** page, where you can place assignments in custom categories and link to the **Create/Edit Categories page**.

Navigation tools

If you have more than 20 students, ThomsonNOW breaks the list into groups of 20 students each and provides **Previous** and **Next** links to help you navigate through the full list.

Gradebook Advanced Options

Click on **Show all commands** to quickly access advanced **Assignment Details** options.

Modify individual student scores/dates

This feature lets you modify the dates and the number of takes for individual students. To change assignments, use the drop-down menu and select the assignment.

Under **Select students for custom assignment dates**, check the box for each student for whom you want to customize dates and takes, scroll down, and click **Continue**.

Search functionality is available if you need to narrow your search by entering in requested student information and clicking **Find Student**.

Under **Students**, select the student(s) you want, and then customize the dates and/or number of takes.

Upon completion, once you've modified all appropriate dates/takes for all selected students, click **Save dates**. This takes you back to the **Assignment Details** page.

E-mail communications center

Lets you communicate with the student quickly without leaving this page.

Edit scores for this assignment

Under **Score Editing**, click **Edit scores for this assignment** to open the **Edit Assignment Details** page. From here you can edit all student scores and custom penalties for an individual.

Upon completion, you can **Save changes and return to Gradebook**, or **Save changes and continue editing**, or **Return to Gradebook without saving**.

Edit all scores on this page/Exit score editing mode

Allows you to change all the scores by displaying **Assignment Score** and **Custom Penalty** or cancels editing mode.

Query Student Data

This takes you to the **Query** page.

Grade Reports

ThomsonNOW Grade Reports give you a quick way to view overall or cumulative course grades, grades for particular assignments, or individual student responses. These reports are generated in file formats that can be printed out, viewed onscreen, or exported to other software (for example, a spreadsheet application) for further editing.

Each of the main pages of the **Gradebook** tab includes a link to the **Report Creator**. For a description of the report types, see "Grade Report Types" on page 54.

Generating Grade Reports

Different reports offer different options you must choose, while some have no options to set. Most reports require that you select basic display options only, such as:

○ How the students are identified (by name, sign-in ID, or student ID)

○ Which assignments to include (for example, past due assignments or assignments not taken)

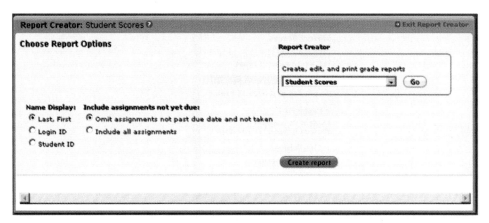

The Report Creator

➢ To create a grade report

1. Once you've selected your report type, set the options for your report, and click **Create report**.

2. Click **Print report** to send a copy of the report, as it appears on your screen, to the printer.

3. To save the report in another format to edit or print, select the format you want, and click **Save report**.

   - **.PDF** reports can be viewed in Adobe® Reader®.

   - **.RTF** reports can be viewed, edited, and printed in Microsoft® Word 2000 (or above) and similar word processor applications.

   - **.TXT** reports are tab-delimited text files that can be viewed in a text editor or opened for viewing in a spreadsheet application (such as Microsoft Excel®).

4. Click **Exit Report Creator** to return to the **Gradebook** page.

Grade Report Types

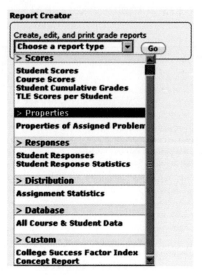

Report types

Scores

Student Scores

For each student, this report displays all the assignments by assignment name, due date, date taken with penalty (if any), percent of total, score, possible score, and the percentage of correct answers. It also provides category totals and overall grade. You can sort the list by student name, sign-in ID, or student ID. This report is a good snapshot of student progress.

Course Scores

This report displays a table listing all assignment grades for all the students enrolled in the course. You can sort the list by student name, sign-in ID, or student ID; numeric score or percentage; assignment name or due date; and you can view adjusted (weighted) or raw scores.

Student Cumulative Grades

This report displays the cumulative score, possible score, and percent correct by category and overall for each student. You can sort the list by student name, sign-in ID, or student ID.

TLE Scores per Student

For TLE assignments, this report displays scores for each student, and includes assignment name, due date, date completed, grade, and time on task. You can sort the list by student name, sign-in ID, or student ID.

Properties

Properties of Assigned Problems

This report lists the assignment's problems by number, ThomsonNOW name, possible score, type, topic, and difficulty rating. It displays the entire range of properties for each item in the selected assignment.

Responses

Student Responses

This report lets you view the problem and answers for one or more students on assignments. It displays the problem, problem type, problem name, student answer, correct answer, and score. This report provides information similar to the problem details found on the **Gradebook** tab.

Student Response Statistics

This report displays the problems in the assignment and provides response statistics for each problem, including percent answering, percent correct, average, and standard deviation and answers for the class. It also displays the problem, problem type, problem name, and correct answer.

Distribution

Assignment Statistics

This report shows student performance and range of scores on the assignment in histogram format. Statistics include number of grades, high/low scores, median, mean, and standard deviation.

Database

All Course & Student Data

This report provides all student grade data for the selected course. You can select the level of detail (course, course section, assignment) and create a spreadsheet-compatible file to view, edit, and print.

Caution: Depending on the number of students, assignments, and level of detail you select, this report can produce a very large output file (4 MB and up).

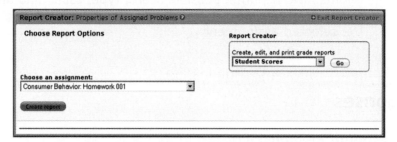

The Report Creator page

CREATING AND MANAGING ASSIGNMENTS

You can easily create and manage a variety of assignments in ThomsonNOW. Depending upon your discipline or course, you may have several sources available for building new assignments. You can create and assign practice quizzes, homework, learning modules, and exams.

Assignments you create are also saved as **Master Files** to allow you to adapt them for other courses or for future users.

- A **Master File** is the set of questions you have chosen for an assignment. Think of it as an unassigned assignment.

- An **Assignment** is the set of questions plus the "assignment options" you assign to a course.

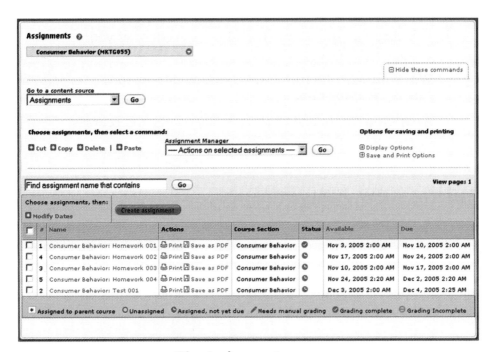

The Assignments page

The Assignments/Tests Tab

To create and manage your assignments, select the **Assignments/Tests** tab, choose the appropriate course, and click **Go**.

Note: To view or create assignments, you must select a course. If you have not yet created a course, or have not been enrolled in one as an instructor, you need to do that first.

Assignments/Tests tab features include:

○ **Creating Assignments**. Create new assignments from your ThomsonNOW **Course Materials** or self-authored questions.

○ **Editing Assignments**. Modify existing assignments for new courses.

○ **Printing Assignments**. Create print versions of your assignments for in-class use.

○ **Working with Master Files**. View, modify, import, or export an existing **Master File**.

○ **Archiving**. Store and retrieve assignments and courses.

Creating New Assignments

The Create Assignment process has a variety of options for building a test or homework assignment or posting a learning module. You have a great amount of control over what is presented to your students, when the assignment is available, and a number of other options available to aid in adapting your assignment to your course.

To Start Creating an Assignment

1. From the **Home** page, click the **Assignments/Tests** tab.

2. Choose the appropriate course from the drop-down menu, and click **Go**.

3. Click the **Create assignment** button. The **Choose content** page opens.

Note: You must select a specific course and/or section before you start to create a new assignment. Once you create your assignment, however, you can assign it to any additional course(s) and/or section(s) you wish.

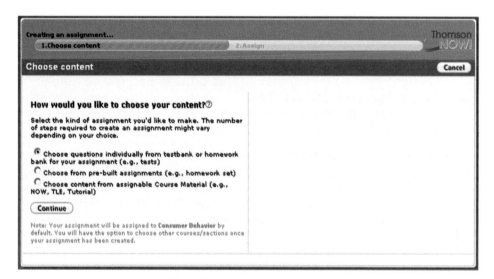

The Choose content page

Choose Assignment Content

The first task in creating an assignment is to choose the content to include in the assignment.

Assignment creation methods

Under **How would you like to choose your content?**, select the option you prefer to use for creating your assignment:

○ **Choose questions individually from test bank or homework bank for your assignment** (**e.g., tests**).
Selecting this option allows you to choose from available question (or test) banks. You will follow a process in which you select chapter(s) and section(s) from which you wish to get question items; filter questions by such things as question type (e.g. Fill in the Blank, Multiple Choice, etc.), concept, and so on; and select the questions you wish to include question by question. After selecting questions you will then be able to set assignment options.

○ **Choose from pre-built assignments** (**e.g., homework set**).
Using this method, you select a complete, ready-made assignment provided with your Thomson textbook. You will be able to delete questions, if you wish, from the pre-built assignment. Following that editing process you will be able to set assignment options. See "Creating a Pre-Built Assignment" on page 92 for the overview and steps for this assignment creation method.

○ **Choose content from assignable Course Material** (**e.g., NOW, TLE, Tutorial**). Using this method, you select a learning module (or modules). Each NOW learning module allows for a pre-test, learning plan, and post-test. Tutorial material, if available with your textbook, is usually accessible by chapter/section. Other courseware content may be available to you. All of these **Course Materials** let you take advantage of questions and assignments that work together as a series. If you select this option, you will be able to select (customize) which parts of the tutorial or learning module will be available to your students. After selecting the appropriate content, you will select the assignment options for all assignments in the sequence. See "Creating an Assignment from Course Material" on page 93 for the overview and steps for this assignment creation method.

Once you have selected the appropriate option, click the **Continue** button. The **Choose content source** selector will open on the right side of the page.

Choose questions individually for your assignment: choosing content sources

Use the **Choose content source** area to select disciplines, books, chapters, sections, and folders from which you want to draw questions or other items for your assignment.

○ Folders with a **+** button contain additional items. Click the **+** button to expand the folder and view the items within.

○ Folders with a **-** button can be collapsed to hide the currently displayed items. Click the **-** button to collapse the folder and hide the items within.

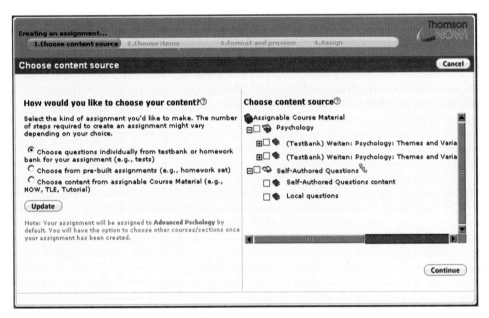

Choosing content sources

You can select from multiple question banks (if available), chapters, sections, and folders from which you want to draw questions or other items for your assignment. When you are finished making your selections, click the **Continue** button.

The types of questions available—based upon what you chose—appears. For example, if the test bank chapter you selected has Multiple Choice, Fill in the Blank, and Matching questions, you will see those listed along with the total number of that question type available.

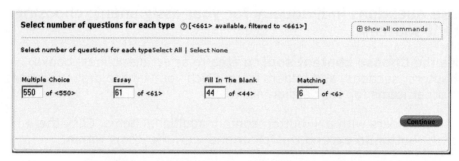

Selecting number of questions for each type

You can click **Select All** to get all the questions available from the content you selected, or you can enter in the available fields how many of each question type you wish to see. For example, if the chapter you selected has 20 Multiple Choice and 20 Matching questions available, and you click **Select All**, you will get all 40 questions to review for inclusion. If you only want the Multiple Choice questions and you want to see all of them, then enter 20 in the field under Multiple Choice and leave 0 in the field below Matching.

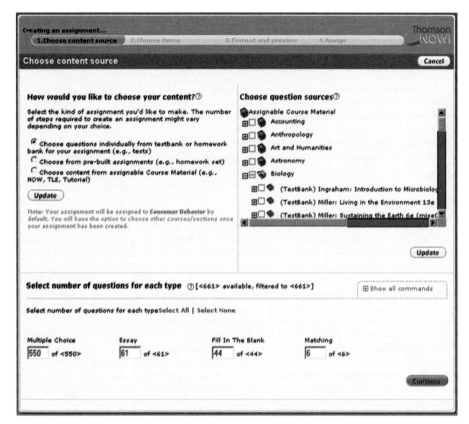

Filtering questions

If you enter a number smaller than the total number available of a particular question type, the number you select for each type will be drawn randomly from those available based upon your source selection and additional filters you may select.

You can click **Select None** to clear all current selections and start over.

Additional filters are available. To access them, click **Show all commands**. If you do not wish to consider other filters for limiting your selected questions, click **Continue**.

Note: If you intend to apply additional filters (see below), you should be aware that it may reduce the total number of questions available. For example, if you select 20 Matching problems and then filter by difficulty level, the 20 problems may be reduced. It is possible to work in reverse order by clicking **Select All**, using additional filters, and then returning to this step to see the available number of each question type.

Using additional filters

The additional filters available depend on the types of questions you have selected for your assignment.

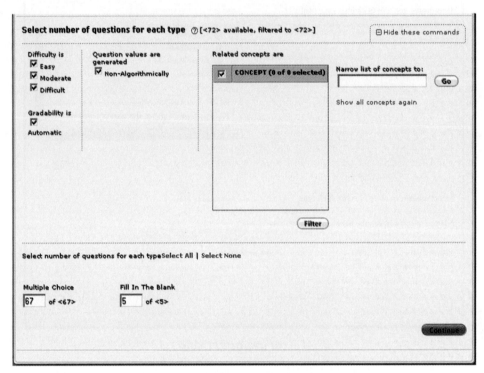

Using additional question filters

Note: Regardless of the number of available questions you draw from initially, please be aware that your finished assignment can have no more than 200 questions. As you apply filters, note the number of questions tally. This **filtered to** number will update each time you change a filter setting and click the **Filter** button.

➤ To apply item filters

1. Make your selections on any filter(s) you wish to apply.

2. Click the **Filter** button to apply and update the filter(s). You can change the settings and refilter the results as much as necessary.

3. When you have applied all of the filters you want, click **Continue** at the bottom. This will take you to the **Review Questions** page.

Filtering by difficulty

This filter allows you the option of choosing questions by their difficulty rating. The difficulty rating of each question is determined by the question's author, and ranges from Easy to Easy-Moderate, Moderate, Moderate-Difficult, and Difficult.

All difficulty ratings are selected by default.

➤ To filter by difficulty

To change the default setting and choose questions with only the difficulty rating that you want, simply:

1. Select the check boxes for the difficulty levels you want to include.

2. Clear the check boxes for the levels you wish to exclude.

3. Click **Filter** to apply your selection.

Filtering by question values

Questions that are authored using algorithms (typically mathematical and statistical questions) can regenerate new values and correct answers each time the question comes up in an online assignment, and each time it is printed (for example as a printed test). This provides great flexibility, enabling you to use the same basic question repeatedly. Conversely, non-algorithmically generated question values appear the same every time they're used.

If included in the content you selected, both types of questions are selected by default.

➤ To filter by question values

To include or exclude questions based on their use of algorithmically generated values:

1. Clear the selection for the type you want to exclude, if any.

2. Click **Filter** to apply your selection to the current set of available problems.

Filtering by gradability

A key feature of ThomsonNOW is that it can electronically grade assignments.

You also have the option of including questions that require manual grading.

- ○ Questions with manual gradability require your subsequent review and grading of every student's work. (These question types might include such things as essay questions.)

- ○ Items that are "not gradable" include non-question items such as readings, illustrations, or comments. (A "not gradable" item is rare in ThomsonNOW.)

All difficulty ratings are selected by default.

➤ To change gradability options

1. Deselect the gradability type(s) you want to exclude.

2. Click **Filter** to apply your selection.

Note: Remember, if you intend to use automatic grading only, you need to clear the selection for **Manual gradability**. Otherwise, you will be required to grade the manually graded problems individually before proceeding with electronic grading for the assignment.

Filtering by related concepts

This filter allows you to select questions by their "related concepts" as defined by the question author. All concepts used in the questions you selected are listed in the **Concepts** box.

All concepts are selected by default.

➤ To change the concepts filter

1. Clear the check boxes to deselect concepts you want to exclude.

2. Type in any specific concept term(s) you want. Click **Show all concepts again** to see the revised concepts list.

3. Once you have selected the concept(s) you want to filter, click **Filter** to apply your selection.

When you have applied all of the filters you want, click the bottom **Continue** button.

Choosing Items for Your Assignment

With all filters selected and applied, you're ready to review the content you have selected, and select the specific questions and other items you want for your assignment.

Once you have the assignment the way you want it, you can assign it to a course, print it, or save it as a **Master File**.

Reviewing and selecting questions

There are two modes in ThomsonNOW for reviewing your questions:

○ **Single List Mode**

○ **Dual List Mode**

These two modes provide the same basic functions, and you can use either one, or both, as you build your assignment. To switch between the two, click the link for the mode you want.

Single List Mode

In **Single List Mode**, all questions are viewable. Included with each question are the source name, grading details, summary information, and a link that allows you to view the question in its electronic (online) form.

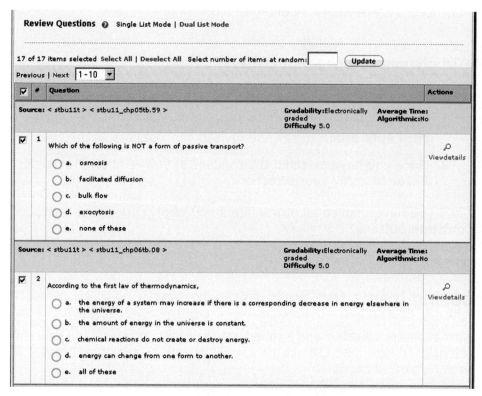

Two questions in Single List Mode

In **Single List Mode**, questions are shown in groups of 10. If you have more than 10 questions, you can use the **Previous** and **Next** links or the drop-down menu to go to the previous or next page of questions.

➢ To select questions in Single List Mode

1. Click the check box(es) to the left of the question(s) you wish to include in your assignment.

   - Use the **Select All** to include all problems, or

   - To draw a specified number of problems at random, enter the number in the **Select number of items at random** box.

2. When the items you want to include are selected, click the **Continue** button at the bottom of the page to proceed.

Dual List Mode

In **Dual List Mode**, problems are listed by their specific file names on two lists. You move the problems you want to include in your assignment from the **choose from problems** list on the left side to the **selected problems** list on the right.

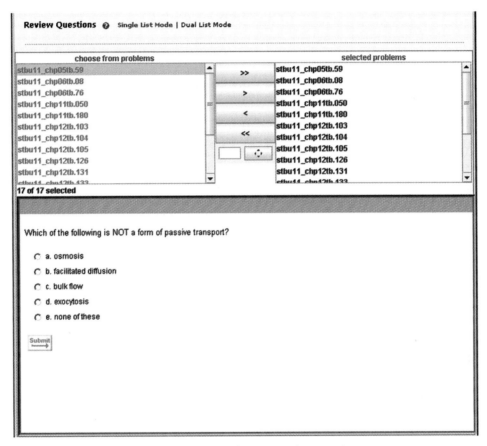

One question in Dual List Mode

The file name typically includes an abbreviation of your textbook's title, chapter, section, and question number. This naming scheme allows for easy correlation between textbook questions and assignment questions. For example, a file name of 01.07.13 would mean this question corresponds to chapter 1, section 7, question 13 in your textbook.

➢ To select questions in Dual List Mode

1. To select or deselect a specific problem, double-click it, OR select it and click the **>** or **<** button.

   - To select or deselect all questions, click **>>** or **<<**.

   - To select questions at random, enter the total number to select and then click the **Update** button.

2. To preview a question, select it in either column and the question will appear at the bottom of the page (scroll down if needed).

3. When all of the items you want to include are selected, click the **Continue** button at the bottom of the page to proceed.

Format and preview the assignment

You **Format and Preview** the assignment while creating it to determine and check its final appearance and behavior. You can also return to this step later to adapt an existing assignment or **Master File** to a new purpose.

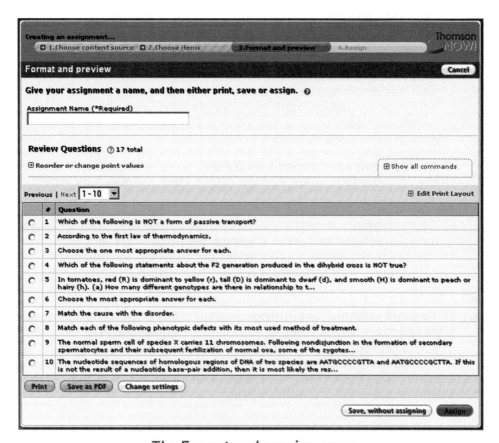

The Format and preview page

This page lets you name the assignment, print it, assign it to a course, or save it as a **Master File**. If you wish, you can reorder the questions, change the score weighting of individual items, or delete items. You can even edit a question's internal authoring and content (recommended for advanced users only).

➢ To name the assignment

1. In the required **Assignment Name** field, type in a name for the assignment. The name has to be unique, and can't use the following characters: backward or forward slashes, colons, asterisks, question marks, quotes, greater-than or less-than symbols, and vertical lines. (\ / : * ? " < > |).

2. If you are satisfied with the content, order, and name of your assignment, the assignment is essentially complete. You have several options available.

○ **To apply online assignment options**. To set up the assignment for online use in a course, click **Assign** and proceed to the **Assignment Options** page.

○ **To print the assignment**. Click the **Print** button to print out your assignment. You will be able to select a header and footer and print the assignment immediately with your current print settings. If needed, you can change font, spacing, and other default print options before printing.

○ **To save the assignment as a PDF**. To save the assignment in the Portable Document Format (PDF), click the **Save as PDF** link.

○ **To change print settings**. To change the default print settings for your assignment, click **Change settings**. This lets you customize the default assignment print layout, including the page headers and footers, problem formatting, typeface, and more.

○ **To save without assigning**. Selecting this option allows you to save your newly created assignment as a **Master File**. You can select this option if you are not yet ready to print your test or to include various online assignment options (e.g., due date). You will be able to access the **Master File** later and use it to create one or more specific assignments.

If there are additional changes you wish to make before proceeding you have a number of options available.

Reordering questions or changing point values

ThomsonNOW provides several options for adjusting the order and score values of your current question set.

Click the **Reorder or change point values** link if you wish to make such changes to your assignment. When you are finished making changes, you can save them and return.

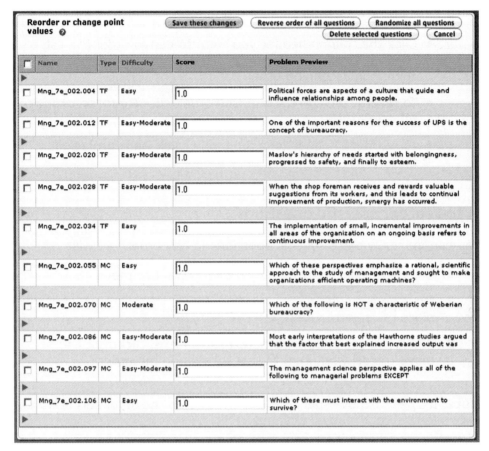

Reordering and changing point values

➤ To change question point values

Most questions are given a default score of 1.0. Changing this value changes the weight of the answer's score relative to the other questions in the assignment. (If you want to weight the whole assignment relative to others, use the **Possible score** or **Grade on a curve** options. See "Choosing Assignment Options" on page 75 for more information.)

- To change and weight the possible score for an individual question, select its **Score** box and type the desired value.

➤ To reorder questions

- Click the column header you want to use to order the list (**Name**, **Type**, or **Difficulty**). The list will be ordered by that column in ascending order.

- To reverse the current question order, click **Reverse order of all questions**.

- To reorder the questions randomly, click **Randomize all questions**.

➤ To reorder specific questions

You can manually place specific questions in any order you wish.

1. Select the check box for the item you want to move.

2. Move your mouse cursor over the line in which you would like to place the selected item.

3. When you see **Insert selected item here**, click that line to move the selected item to that location in the order.

Note: It's best to move specific questions last, as the other sort features may override your manual changes.

➤ To delete specific questions

1. Select the question(s) you want to delete.

2. Click **Delete selected questions**.

When the assignment questions' scoring and order are the way you want them, click **Save these changes** to save them and return to the **Format and preview** page. To abandon your changes, click **Cancel** instead.

Additional format and preview tasks

The following commands allow you to make additional changes to your assignment before proceeding. To access them, click the **Show all commands** link.

○ **Question clipboard.** Use these commands to **Cut**, **Copy**, **Delete** or **Paste** selected questions on the list.

○ **Manage Questions.** These links provide ways for you to add to or change your current questions without starting over.

- **Author new question.** Click this link to author your own ThomsonNOW question from scratch and insert it into this assignment. You will name the question, choose its problem type, and then create it in the appropriate authoring editor (recommended for advanced users only). See "Authoring in ThomsonNOW" on page 133 for details.

- **Edit a selected question.** Use this link to open the currently selected question in the appropriate ThomsonNOW authoring editor to change its internal logic and grading (recommended for advanced users only). See "Authoring in ThomsonNOW" on page 133 for details.

- **Add more questions.** This option essentially repeats the Create Assignment process for the purpose of selecting one or more questions to add to your current assignment. You will choose content sources, filter questions, and review your additions before they are added.

○ **View Mode.** This option lets you see the assignment from the student's point of view.

- **Student View**. This option lets you preview the selected question as it will appear to the student online.

Choosing Assignment Options

Assignment options let you create different kinds of assignments customized for the needs of your courses and your students. You can allow a homework assignment to be taken an unlimited number of times, for example, and a final exam only once. In addition to dates, times, and scoring, you can allow or disallow such things as hints, solutions, and feedback (if available). You can even allow students to retake only those questions they miss.

Note: You can set the assignment options while creating the assignment as described here, or set them later to adapt an existing assignment or **Master File** (a set of questions) to a new purpose. Setting the options essentially turns a **Master File** into a "live" assignment with defined due date, grading rules, students, and feedback.

Editing assignment options

You can choose the various assignment options individually, or as a predefined "option set" that you have saved previously.

➢ To edit assignment options

You will typically set an assignment's options when you first create the assignment. If you are creating a set of assignments, you can enter the options for all assignments at one time. You can also edit the assignment's options after it has been assigned to a course.

1. From the **Assignments** list, click on the assignment you want to edit.

2. From the **View/Edit an Assignment** window, click the **Modify assignment options** link.

3. Make the appropriate settings for the assignment. (To see all of the available options, click the **Show all options** link.)

4. When you have all the settings the way you want them, click the **Save** button at the bottom of the page.

Using assignment option sets

You can save your preferred assignment options as an option set and then apply this saved set to new assignments. Using option sets helps you create new assignments more quickly and apply options more consistently even as you create assignments ranging from practice exercises to exams.

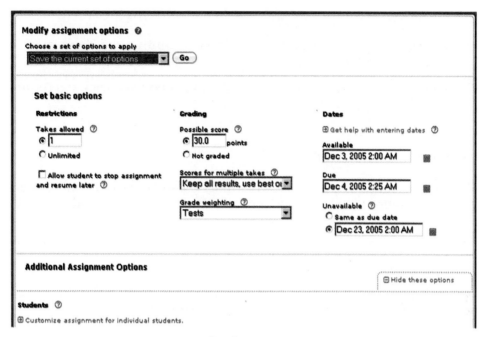

Option sets

For example, you can configure one option set as a homework template that allows multiple attempts, unlimited time frame, and feedback hints. You can create another set for a quiz that allows only one attempt, a limited time frame, and penalties for using hints.

➤ To create a new option set

1. In the **Modify Assignment Options** page, edit the basic and additional options as needed.

2. On the **Choose a set of options to apply** drop-down menu, click **Save the current set of options**, and then click **Go**.

3. When prompted, enter a name for your new option set, and then click **OK**

4. Make your changes to specific options, and then click the **Save** button at the bottom of the page.

➤ To make permanent changes to an existing option set

1. From the **Choose a set of options to apply** drop-down menu, select the option set you wish to change.

2. Make your changes to specific options, and then click the **Save** button at the bottom of the page.

Basic assignment options

The initial **Assign** page provides the most commonly used options. For additional, more advanced assignment options, click **Show all options**.

Restrictions

Takes allowed

You can set a limit on how many times students can take an assignment. The default setting is **Unlimited**.

To specify a number of allowed "takes" (attempts), select the **Takes allowed** radio button, and then enter the number of desired takes in the adjacent box.

Unlimited

Select the **Unlimited** radio button to allow the student unlimited takes of the assignment.

Allow student to stop assignment and resume later

Select this check box to let students stop work on an assignment, save their work, and resume the assignment later. To require that students start and finish the assignment in one session (e.g., for an exam), clear (de-select) the check box.

Note: If you allow students to save and resume, the additional assignment option **Time allowed** must remain as **Unlimited**.

Grading

Possible score

The **Possible score** is the number of points the student can earn from the assignment. An assignment's default score is typically 1 point per question. For example, an assignment with 10 questions has a default score of 10 points.

You can also use the **Possible score** to define a different score. For example, you might want a possible score of 25 points for the assignment. This provides a way to change the importance or weighting of the assignment in calculating the course grade.

Note: Other functions that allow assignment weighting are **Grade Weighting** and **Assignment Categories**.

Not graded

To indicate that an assignment does not contribute any points or score to the course grade, select **Not graded**.

Scores for multiple takes

There are several options for how to select and calculate a student's score when you have allowed students to take the assignment more than once.

- **Keep one result, overwrite on each take**. Only the most recent result for the entire assignment (including questions not answered) will be kept. This is the default setting.

- **Keep one result, merge on each take** (also known as "merge mode"). All correctly answered questions will be kept as soon as a student submits the assignment. Only those questions the student missed will appear on subsequent takes. This allows students to keep taking the same test with new questions until they have answered all questions correctly or until they have reached the maximum number of times allowed. An assignment set up this way A) allows students to take an assignment over multiple sessions and B) lets students gain feedback from both errors and correct answers while ensuring that they can't cheat by copying answers into retakes.

Note: Selecting merge mode automatically sets **Regenerate question values** to **Never**.

- This means that questions with algorithmically generated values will not be reset to new values each time the student takes the test. In other words, the question will appear the same way every time.

- If you do want the student to see a new version of the question every time, you can set **Regenerate question values** to **On each take**. This will present each question with new values for every take.

- Selecting merge mode also sets **Show correct answers** to **Hide correct answers**. This means that students who view their score details after taking the assignment will not see the correct answers for the questions they missed. (This prevents students from copying down the correct answers before taking the assignment again.)

- If you select merge mode, it is also recommended that you limit the **Attempts allowed per question** to **1** or **2**.

- **Keep all results, use best one**. All results for all questions will be kept. The grade will be calculated using the assignment with the best overall grade. The multiple results are displayed in the **Gradebook** score details, with the best score highlighted.

- **Keep all results, use last one**. All results for all questions will be kept. The grade will be calculated using only the most recent set of results. The multiple results are displayed in the **Gradebook** score details, with the last score highlighted.

- **Keep all results, merge on each take**. This option lets you save all of a student's takes for viewing in **Grade Details**. Correct answers are merged (accumulated) from each take to determine the assignment grade, while subsequent takes require students to answer only the questions he or she missed on previous attempts. The multiple results are displayed in bar graph format in the **Gradebook** score details, with the merged score highlighted. This option sets **Regenerate items** to **Never** and **Show correct answers** to **Hide correct answers**.

Categories

Use this drop-down menu to select a grade-weighting category for the assignment.

The categories you create let you group assignments to weight them collectively in final grade calculations. For example, you can create a category containing homework assignments and weight it to equal 30% of the course grade. This weighting will apply whether the category has 5 or 50 homework assignments.

- To create or edit your grade-weighting categories, select **Edit weighting categories…**.

- If you have not created any categories, or don't want to select a category, select **Default**.

Dates

Available

Use this box to enter the date and time that students can begin the assignment. Click the adjacent **Calendar** icon, select the appropriate date and time, and then click **Set date** to fill in the date field. You can also type the date and time directly if you use the ThomsonNOW date formats.

Due

Use this field to enter the assignment's **Due** date and time. After the **Due** date, students will be unable to start, resume, or complete the assignment in progress (unless you also have entered a **Late Penalty**).

If a student is working on the assignment when the **Due** date and time passes, the assignment will be stopped and scored on progress to that point. If you want to allow students to complete the assignment after the **Due** date, you must set a **Late Penalty**.

Click the adjacent **Calendar** icon, select the appropriate date and time, and then click **Set date** to fill in the date field. You can also type the date and time directly if you use the ThomsonNOW date formats.

Unavailable

Assignments normally become unavailable after the **Due** date (unless you have set up a **Late Penalty**). You can set a date and time other than the **Due** date to make the assignment unavailable for students to take.

- To have the assignment's **Unavailable** date be the same as the **Due** date, select **Same as due date**.

- To specify an **Unavailable** date that differs from the **Due** date, select the text box. Click the adjacent **Calendar** icon, select the appropriate date and time, and then click **Set date** to fill in the date field.

Additional assignment options

You can access the **Additional Assignment Options** on the **Assign** page or **Modify Assignments Options** page by clicking the **Show all options** link. In general, these additional options are more specialized and advanced than the basic default options.

Note: These options can provide powerful teaching tools, but you may want to experiment before you "go live" with your assignments. Create a small "play test" or a set of small assignments. You can then try out, for example, the grading or prerequisite settings to see what works best for your course.

Students

Customize assignment for individual students

This link opens a page that lets you tailor the settings for this assignment for particular students within the course.

Once you have opened the **Modify individual student scores/ dates** page, use the **Students** column to select those students to whom you want to apply the subsequent date or takes settings on this page.

You can also customize the following assignment options (described below) on a student-by-student basis.

Available

Enter the **Available** date and time on which students can begin the assignment. Select **Use default** to use the default available date and time currently assigned to the course, or enter a new date and time for the selected student(s).

Due

Enter the assignment **Due** date and time for the selected student(s). Select **Use default** to use the default date/time currently assigned to the course, or enter a new date and time for the selected student(s).

Unavailable

Enter the assignment's **Unavailable** date and time for the selected student(s) (if different from the **Due** date). Select **Use default** to use the default unavailable date and time currently assigned to the course, or enter a new date and time for the selected student(s).

Maximum Takes Allowed

You can specify the maximum number of times a student can take the assignment. Select **Use default** to use the number set for the course, or enter a new number of takes for the selected student(s) in the adjacent field.

Restrictions (additional)

Time allowed per take

This field allows you to set a time limit for every take (attempt) for the assignment.

- **Unlimited**. Select this check box to allow students unlimited time to complete the assignment (until the **Due** date and time are passed).

- **Minutes**. Select this check box to specify a time limit for each take of the assignment, and then enter the allotted time, in minutes, in the adjacent entry box.

Require password to take

There might be times when you will want to define a password for an assignment. Any student trying to start this assignment will be prompted for the password, and will have to enter it correctly to proceed. This option lets you set up assignments (such as final exams) that can be taken only after you have given students the password. It's a good way to ensure that students do not take this assignment until a specified time.

Prerequisite

You can prevent students from taking an assignment until specified criteria are met. The value you enter for this property (formerly known as "Condition") is an expression that defines these limits for each student. See the ThomsonNOW online Help for examples.

If prerequisite is not met

If you set a **Prerequisite** for this assignment, you must also choose what to do when the **Prerequisite** tests "false" (that is, students cannot complete the assignment because they have not met the prerequisite). You can use these properties (formerly known as "Condition Mode") to create customized lesson plans for different kinds of students.

- **Students can see but cannot take assignment.** Selecting this option makes the assignment visible to students who cannot take it because they have not met the condition specified by the **Prerequisite** property. This is an appropriate setting for assignments you want students to be able to study in detail before completing (such as homework, or perhaps an open-book test).

- **Assignment is not visible, but counts towards grade**. Selecting this option makes the assignment not visible to students who have not met the condition specified by the **Prerequisite** property, but the assignment does count toward their grade. This is an appropriate setting for assignments whose details you do not want students to know in advance (such as most tests, or homework that might not make sense before the condition is met).

- **Assignment does not count towards student's grade**. The assignment is not visible to students, and is not counted in their grade unless they meet the condition specified by the **Prerequisite** option. Once they meet the **Prerequisite** and "unlock" the assignment, however, the assignment becomes visible, must be taken, and counts towards their grade. This setting is useful if you want students to demonstrate proficiency before proceeding.

Allow printing before this assignment is taken

Select this check box to allow students to print the assignment prior to clicking **Take**.

Description

In the **Public, seen by students** field, you can enter comments for students to read when they take the assignment.

Notes

The **Private, unseen by students** field is where you can enter comments that are viewable only by yourself or by another instructor. Such comments might include cautions about manually graded items, a summary of the assignment setup, or any other information you want other instructors to be able to use within the assignment. This field is particularly useful if you are teaching a large course with sections taught by other instructors.

Grading (additional)

Curve

You can give this assignment a value to increase or decrease the effect of its grade on the student's overall grade. The assignment grade is multiplied by the specified value (the default is 1.0). So, for example, if you enter 1.25 for an assignment that has a possible score of 8 points, a student who answered all questions correctly would receive 10 points.

You can use **Curve** to weight assignments in calculating the final grade. Other functions that allow assignment weighting are **Possible score** and **Assignment Categories**.

Pass/Fail

To grade an assignment as **Pass/Fail** (or "pass /no pass") enter the minimum percentage score required to pass the assignment. For example, on a 10-point quiz, a **Pass/Fail** value of 65% would mark any score of 6.5 or more as a **Pass** and anything less as a **Fail**. Any **Pass** score will receive full credit (100%) for the assignment, and any **Fail** score will receive no credit (0%). Using the same example, a passing student score of 6.5 would receive 100% credit (10 points) for the assignment, while a failing score of 5.0 would receive 0% credit (0 points) for the assignment. If the **Pass/Fail** entry is set to 0 (the default setting), the assignment is scored normally.

Extra credit

You can choose to make this assignment available for extra credit only. To do so, simply select the **Extra credit** check box.

Late Penalty

Select the check box for **Late Penalty** to assess a grade penalty for late assignments. You can then use one or both of the following selections to define the penalty as a fixed and/or accumulating amount:

Penalty applied immediately after due date

Use this box to enter a flat penalty for completing the assignment after the **Due** date/time. Enter the penalty as a decimal (0.0 to 1.0) or as a percentage (0% to 100%), where 0 represents full credit. Example: Enter 0.25 to penalize the score 25% if taken after the **Due** date.

Subsequent penalty

Use this box to enter a penalty that accumulates by how late the assignment is submitted. Enter the penalty as a decimal (0.0 to 1.0) or as a percentage (0% to 100%), where 0 represents full credit. Then use the radio button selector under **Apply subsequent penalty every** to indicate whether the penalty is to be assessed per **Hour**, **Day**, or **Week** late. Example: Enter 0.1 per additional week to increase the penalty 10% per week after the **Due** date.

The subsequent penalty does not begin to accumulate until the end of the first hour, day, or week. To assess an accumulating penalty that begins immediately, enter the penalty in the **Penalty applied immediately after due date** box as well.

Note: You can also manually adjust a **Late Penalty** in the **Gradebook** later, should special circumstances require it.

Grading Mode

You may be able to choose how strictly to grade answers for electronically graded Free Response and Fill in the Blank problems with numeric answers. Whether or not you can use this option depends on how the problem was originally authored. The options are:

Authored

The problem will be graded exactly as it was originally authored.

Loose

The problem will be graded less strictly than as authored. In most authored problems, ThomsonNOW's sophisticated Computer Algebra System accommodates the appropriate range of answer variants for individual test bank and homework items. **Loose** grading allows a somewhat broader range of acceptable answers.

Loose grading substitutes the "value" grading method for whatever grading method was authored for the item. The value method performs a numerical substitution of random values for all parameters in the correct answer and the student's answer. If all calculations are equal, the student's answer is scored as correct.

Numerical tolerance

Enter the appropriate percentage value for the tolerance you want in the correct answer. The value 0 means that no deviation is allowed. The value 100 means that the allowed deviation is equal to the absolute value of the correct answer. For example, a tolerance setting of 1% for an answer of -300 will allow an answer of +/- 3, or anything from -297 to 303.

Questions

Regenerate question values

Most ThomsonNOW questions are authored to include a range of variable values. This lets you regenerate new versions of the questions for each student attempt (if you allow multiple attempts for assignments) or for each student. Your options are:

- **On each take**. This option will create new versions of questions each time a student takes the assignment. This means that different students will see different versions of the questions and that the questions will change each time they take the assignment.

Note: You can select **Regenerate on each take** when **Merge Mode** is selected for the **Track Multiple Results** property.

- **Once per student**. This option creates a unique set of question values for each student, and presents those same values each time the student takes the assignment. In other words, different students will see different versions of the questions, but they will see those same questions every time they take the assignment.

- **Never**. This option will present the same questions to all students for each take of the assignment. In other words, all students will see the same questions each time. This is the default setting.

Shuffle questions on every take

You can choose whether or not to have the system create a different order for the items on this assignment each time it is generated. By default, questions won't be shuffled.

Selecting this option will randomly shuffle items each time the assignment is generated. Shuffling items is useful if you are concerned about students copying answers from each other without even bothering to read the questions or handing out answers to, for example, "question 7."

Note: If you create an assignment in which items build on previous items, do not shuffle your questions.

Attempts allowed per question

You can allow students to attempt each question multiple times before they submit the entire assignment, regardless of how many times you allow them to submit the assignment itself.

- To specify a number of attempts, select **Attempts allowed per question** and enter the appropriate number in the box.

- To allow an unlimited number, select **Unlimited**.

Note: If you choose to have feedback (rejoinders) displayed for multiple attempts, you can also choose whether to deduct points for using feedback from the student's grade. See the **Feedback during assignment** property.

Penalize multiple attempts

Select this check box to penalize the student's score on a problem for each unsuccessful attempt to answer it. This penalty will apply regardless of any additional settings for **Question attempts before hints** or **Attempts before feedback**.

With **Penalize multiple attempts** enabled, each time the student attempts the problem and gets it wrong, the possible score for that problem is multiplied by its penalty factor as follows.

- **Penalty Factor: 0.9 per attempt (10% penalty)**. Problem types: MultiAnswer, Sketch3D, SpreadSheet.

- **Penalty Factor: 0.75 per attempt (25% penalty)**. Problem types: ChemConstructor, Dnd, EnergyLevels, FITB, Flash, GeomObjects, Notebook, SimpleTable, SingleAnswer, SpectrumHotSpot, TextHighlighter, TutorialProblem, VennDiagram.

- **Penalty Factor: 0.5 per attempt (50% penalty)**. Problem types: ChemChooser, HotSpot, Matching, MC, ModifiedTF.

- **Penalty Factor: 0.0 per attempt (100% penalty)**. Problem types: True False, DND2.

Note: The penalty factor for a particular problem depends on the problem type, as defined internally by ThomsonNOW. It cannot be adjusted by the instructor or problem author.

Automatically advance to next question

You can choose how to have the system advance to the next question after students submit an answer.

- **Don't auto-advance**. Students must manually select the next question to answer.

- **When any answer is submitted**. (Default selection.) The system automatically advances after every submitted question. Note that this option disables feedback (rejoinders).

- **When correct answer is submitted**. The system automatically advances only if the student has submitted a correct answer.

Presentation and feedback

These options control how individual items, hints, and feedback are presented.

Style of presentation

Use this drop-down menu to select some aspects of how the assignment appears and is controlled.

- **Homework: progress/takes meters**. Displays the assignment to the student with a current progress/score meter and a "takes" counter (for assignments allowing multiple takes).

- **Test: no onscreen meters**. Displays the assignment without the progress/score meter or "takes" counter.

- **Tutorial**. Displays the assignment using the tutorial interface. Tutorial-style assignments that are built from existing tutorial content can link to related materials such as reading, videos, or exercises from the source tutorial.

Feedback during assignment

Select this check box to display any available feedback (default or custom) for the question, and to enable the following set of feedback options.

Show feedback in pop-up window

Select this check box to display any available feedback (default or custom) in a new pop-up window.

Question attempts before hints

If hints are available for items you include in this assignment, you can specify how many times students attempt a question before a hint appears.

- **No hints**. Select this radio button to allow no hints to appear.

- To allow hints after a specified number of attempts, select the second radio button and enter the desired number of attempts in the adjacent box.

Note: If you do not enter a value for this option, available hints will appear before students attempt a question. (Not all questions have hints. Hints can be created only when the question is originally authored, or when the authoring is edited.)

Attempts before feedback

If feedback (default or custom) is available for items you include in this assignment, you can specify how many times students attempt a question before feedback appears.

- **No feedback**. Select this radio button to allow no feedback to appear.

- To allow feedback after a specified number of attempts, select the second radio button and enter the desired number of attempts in the adjacent box.

Note: The default feedback message simply informs the student if an answer is correct or incorrect. More specific feedback is provided only if the authored content for the item includes it.

Display time left warning at

If you have set a time limit for this assignment, you can enter the time after which a warning message will appear to notify students of the time remaining to complete the assignment.

- **No warning**. Select this radio button to show no on-screen warning as the assignment time nears its end.

- To enable a warning after a specified number of minutes, select the second radio button and enter the desired number of minutes in the adjacent box. For example, for a 5-minute warning on a 1-hour assignment, enter 55; the warning will appear 55 minutes into the assignment.

Note: You must enter the time allowed in the appropriate format. See "Date/Time Formatting" on page 32.

Feedback after assignment

Select this check box to let students see feedback on their assignment results. You can then choose from the following set of feedback options.

Results to display

Use these settings to control what results students can see once they complete the assignment.

- **Scores**. Shows students only assignment-level summary information about their grade for the assignment.

- **Scores & details**. Shows students how they scored on each item in the assignment, as well as assignment-level summary information.

- **Scores, details & correct answers**. Shows students the correct answers for answers they missed. Also shows how they scored on each item in the assignment, and summary information.

When to make results available

Use this setting to control when students can view their results. For example, you may want students to see full assignment and item details right away for a practice assignment. On the other hand, you may never want them to view the results for a final exam or after a specified date for quizzes and tests.

- **Immediately after take**. Select this radio button to let students see assignment results as soon they submit their work.

- To let students see their results only after a specified date and time, select the second radio button and enter the desired date and time in the adjacent box with the **Calendar** tool, or enter it directly using the ThomsonNOW date/time formats.

Enable printing when there are more takes

Use this setting to allow students to print an assignment with more takes allowed. For instance, a student might print an assignment to work on it away from the computer and enter answers later.

When you have your **Basic** assignment options set the way you want them (and **Additional** options, if any) click **Save** to save the assignment and view your **Assignment summary**.

Creating a Pre-Built Assignment

This section describes the process of creating an assignment from a pre-built (or "form") assignment drawn directly from your ThomsonNOW books or courseware. Pre-built assignments allow you to take advantage of pre-designed question sets that match your textbook chapters and sections.

In this process, you start with a complete, ready-made assignment provided with your Thomson textbook, but you can then review, remove or reorder its questions. Once you have selected your questions, you can set the specific assignment options, such as due date, grading, hint availability, and other settings. When you have finished creating the assignment, you can edit all aspects of its contents and formatting.

➤ To create a pre-built assignment

1. On your **Assignments/Tests** page, select the course for which you want to create the pre-built assignment, and click the adjacent **Go** button.

2. Click the **Create assignment** button.

3. Under **How would you like to choose your content?**, select the second option **Choose from pre-built assignments (e.g., homework set)**. Click the **Continue** button.

4. Under **Choose content source**, find your registered ThomsonNOW book or courseware from which you want to select the pre-built assignment. Pre-built assignments typically correspond to your book chapters.

5. Click on the **+/-** buttons next to each listed item to view/hide its contents. Select (check) the assignment you want to use. Click the **Continue** button just below.

    Note: You can select only one pre-built assignment at a time.
    ---

6. You will go immediately to the **Assign** page, where you can set the **Basic** and **Additional** assignment options such as number of takes, due date, and scoring. For details on the individual options available for your assignment, see "Choosing Assignment Options" on page 75.

7. Once you have the options set to your liking, click the **Save** button at the bottom of the page. The assignment is now created, saved, and assigned.

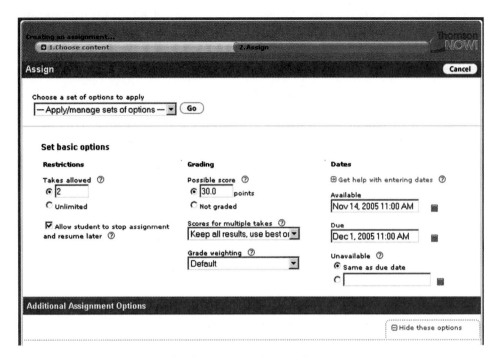

Assigning pre-built assignment

If you wish, you may now access the finished assignment from the **View/Edit Assignments** page to edit or reorder its questions, change formatting, and customize its print options. See "Editing Assignments" on page 99 for details.

Creating an Assignment from Course Material

You can create graded assignments from your ThomsonNOW self-study course materials, including NOW, TLE, or tutorial courseware. You can create a single assignment, or a whole series at once.

Assignments you create from the self-study tutorial materials included with the student's textbook can include diagnostic pre-tests, interactive content, and a post-test (chapter quiz) to assess your students' grasp of the material. **Course materials** assignments allow you to assign entire sets of interactive content quickly, as well as track and grade each student's work.

Once you have selected your questions, you can set a limited number of assignment options, such as due dates for the whole series. When you have finished creating the assignments, you can edit all aspects of their contents and formatting.

Note: Once students register the **Content Access Code** for their textbook, they can access **Course Material** content on their own on an ungraded, self-study basis. Be sure they understand that they must complete the assignments from their **Assignments/Tests** tab to receive assignment credit in your course.

➢ To create an assignment from Course Material content

1. On your **Assignments/Tests** tab, select the course for which you want to create the assignment(s), and click the adjacent **Go** button.

2. Click the **Create assignment** button.

3. Under **How would you like to choose your content?**, select the third option **Choose content from assignable Course Material (e.g., NOW, TLE, Tutorial)**. Click the **Continue** button just below.

4. Under **Choose content source**, find your registered ThomsonNOW discipline, book, and courseware from which you want to create the assignment(s), and find the appropriate chapter(s). Click on the **+/-** buttons next to an item to view/hide its contents. Select (check) the chapter(s) you want to use, and then click the **Continue** button just below.

   - If you select just one courseware chapter, you will go directly to the **Customize Content** page. (See "Customizing content" on page 95 for more information.) Depending on the chapter content, you can then rename the assignment, and include/exclude specific chapter sections including the diagnostic **Pre-Test** and **Post-Test**. Once you have customized content for the assignment, click the **Continue** button to proceed to the **Assign** page and set assignment options.

   - If you select multiple courseware chapters, you will see a dialog box informing you that you have selected multiple assignments, and will be setting assignment options next. Required settings include the **Available** and **Due** dates, and **Days between due dates**. (See "Setting options for multiple

Course Material assignments" on page 96 for more information.) Click the **OK** button to proceed. You will then go directly to the **Assign** page, where you can set the **Basic** and **Additional** assignment options. Once you have set the options for the assignment set, click the **Save** button.

5. At this point, your assignment or set of assignments is complete and assigned to the current course. However, you still have the ability to modify the assignment(s) as you wish from the **View/ Edit Assignment** page.

- **Modify assignment options**. Return to the **Modify assignment options** page to fine-tune the options settings for the selected assignment(s).

- **Assign to other course/section**. Click this link to assign the selected material to another one of your existing courses or sections.

- **Customize content**. Click this link to change an assignment name, include/exclude pre-tests and scores, or include/ exclude specific sections. (See "Customizing content," below.)

- **Take this assignment offline**. Makes the assignment **Unavailable** to students until you return it to **Online** status. This is a recommended step if you need to make changes to live assignments.

Customizing content

When you are creating **Course Materials** assignments from a single chapter, or editing one later from **View/Edit Assignments**, you can use the **Customize Content** page to select a name and specific chapter sections.

○ Use the **Assignment Name** field to review the assignment name, or rename if needed.

○ Use the radio buttons to choose if you want to include the chapter diagnostic **Pre-Test**, the **Post-Test** "chapter quiz," or both. If you include the **Pre-Test**, you can then choose whether to record the score.

◯ Use the check boxes to include or exclude specific chapter content sections from the assignment.

When you have customized the assignment content to your liking, click **Continue** to proceed to the **Assignment Options** page (when creating the assignment) or **Save** to return to **View/Edit Assignments** (when editing the assignment later).

Setting options for multiple Course Material assignments

When you are creating **Course Materials** assignments from multiple chapters, you set the **Available** and **Due** dates for the entire assignment series, and can set other assignment options as well. You can also modify the options for individual assignments later from **View/ Edit Assignments**.

On the **Assign** page, you will set the following options:

- Under **Dates**, note the **First Assignment Available** and **Due** date settings. Once you set these dates for the first assignment in the group, set the number of days allowed for taking each subsequent assignment in the required **Days between due dates** box. Using this setting, ThomsonNOW will automatically set the **Available/Due** dates for the entire group of assignments. (You can change these later if needed.)

- To include weekend days on the days allowed for each assignment, click the **Allow dates on weekend** check box.

Note: Course Materials assignments have many of their options selected already. Accordingly, you will see fewer **Additional** options to set than you would with the other assignment types.

For details on the other individual options available for your assignment, see "Choosing Assignment Options" on page 75. Once you have the assignment options set to your liking, click the **Save** button at the bottom right of the page.

Creating an External Assignment

This section describes the process of creating an External assignment from one of your existing assignments.

In this process, you start by creating a **WebQuiz** from the assignment's **Master File**. This generates your assignment's URL (web address.) You then return to the **Assignments** list, create the External assignment, and specify the assignment options. When you have finished creating the assignment, you can edit all aspects of its contents and formatting.

➢ To create an External assignment

1. Create a **WebQuiz** using the assignment **Master File**. See "Creating a WebQuiz" on page 124 for the procedure. Before you leave the **Master Files** page, select the file and click the **WebQuiz properties** link. Copy the entire URL into your system clipboard.

2. On your **Assignments/Tests** page, select the course for which you want to create the assignment(s), and click the adjacent **Go** button.

3. Click the **Show all commands** link.

4. Check the assignment you want to make available externally (accessible from the web, outside ThomsonNOW).

5. From the **Assignment Manager** drop-down menu, select **Create External**, and then click the adjacent **Go** button.

6. On the **Give your assignment a name** page, enter the name you want to use for this External assignment in the **Assignment Name** box.

7. In the **URL** box, paste the generated URL (valid web address) you copied from your **WebQuiz** properties for the assignment.

8. If you want, you can use the **Description** box to enter (or paste) a plain text description of the assignment that will be visible to students as they select and start the assignment.

9. Click the **Save** button.

10. On the **Set your assignment options** page, you can set more assignment options such as **Grading** and **Due** date, as well as additional options available for External assignments (click **Show all options**.) For details on the individual options available for your assignment, see "Choosing Assignment Options" on page 75.

11. Once you have the options set to your liking, click the **Save** button at the bottom right of the page.

Your **Assignments** page will open with the external assignment now listed, assigned, and ready to take. If you wish, you may now review the finished assignment to edit the questions, reformat, or modify print settings. You can also reorder or delete assignments as needed. See "Editing Assignments" on page 99 for details.

Creating a Comment Assignment

This section describes how to create a stand-alone **Comment** to provide information to your students on their **Assignments** list. You can set up the **Comment** to be viewed by particular students only, or those meeting certain prerequisites (completion of a certain assignment, for example).

You create **Comments** on the **Assignments/Tests** page. When you have finished creating the **Comment**, you can edit its contents, student access, and other options.

➢ To create a Comment assignment

1. On your **Assignments/Tests** page, select the course for which you want to create the **Comment**, and click the adjacent **Go** button.

2. Click the **Show all commands** link.

3. From the **Assignment Manager** drop-down menu, select **Create Comment**, and then click the adjacent **Go** button.

4. On the **Give your assignment a name** page, enter the name you want to use for this **Comment** in the **Assignment Name** box. In the **Comment** box, enter (or paste) your plain text **Comment** that will be displayed to students when they "take" the **Comment** assignment.

5. Click the **Save** button.

6. On the **Set your assignment options** page, you can set more assignment options for the **Comment**. All are optional.

   • **Date**. Sets the last date on which the **Comment** can be viewed.

- **Students**. Allows you to specify particular students who can view or not view the **Comment**.

- **Prerequisites**. Allows you to set a prior condition for viewing the **Comment**, such as registered book access or a passing score on a previous assignment. See "Restrictions" on page 78 for more detail on how prerequisites work.

7. The main setting is the date on which the **Comment** is "due" (must be viewed) such as due dates, as well as additional options available for external assignments (click **Show all options**). For details on the individual options available for your assignment, see "Choosing Assignment Options" on page 75

8. Once you have the options set to your liking, click the **Save** button at the bottom right of the page.

   Your **Assignments** page will open with the **Comment** listed and ready to view (for the appropriate students). Students who meet the **Comment**'s conditions (if any) can simply click the **Comment** view icon to see it.

   If you wish, you may edit the finished **Comment** to change its text or options.

Editing Assignments

Once you have created an assignment or **Master File**, you can still modify almost every aspect of its content, appearance, or behavior. For example, you can add questions, reorder items, change the due dates, scoring, or other options, or even re-author current questions. In many cases, you may find yourself copying a proven assignment and editing parts of it to suit a new class.

Viewing/Editing Assignments

You can view and edit any assignment listed on your **Assignments/Tests** page. Simply click on the assignment name to go to the **View/Edit an Assignment** page for that assignment.

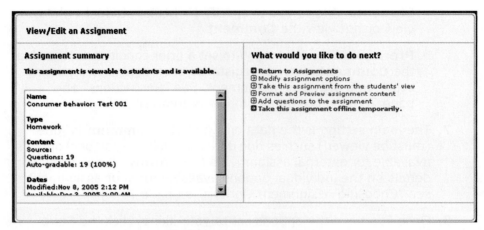

Editing an assignment

Note: If the assignment's current status is **Assigned, not yet due**, you may want to take it offline while you are working on it. In addition, you should consider if changes to the assignment will affect students who have already taken it, or affect class grading overall.

The **View/Edit an Assignment** page has the following links:

Return to Assignments

Returns you to the main **Assignments/Tests** page.

Modify assignment options

Opens the **Modify assignment options** page for the assignment, allowing you to reconfigure assignment due dates, scoring, grading, assignees, and other assignment behavior. See "Choosing Assignment Options" on page 75.

Take this assignment from the students' view

Loads the assignment and allows you to take it, start to finish, from the student's point of view. This lets you test the assignment and verify that the content, hints, scoring, and so on, work as intended. Your results will not be recorded in the **Gradebook**, however.

Format and Preview assignment content

Opens the assignment in the **Format and preview** page, where you can rename the assignment or work with its question order and point values. See "Format and preview the assignment" on page 70 for more information.

Add questions to the assignment

Lets you gather new questions from your Thomson books or self-authored questions to add to the assignment, with the same process used to create the assignment. See "Creating New Assignments" on page 58.

Take this assignment offline temporarily.

Make this assignment temporarily unavailable to your students.

Additional assignment commands

Access the following commands from the **Format and preview** page by clicking **Show all commands**.

Question clipboard

Use these commands to **Cut**, **Copy**, **Delete**, or **Paste** selected questions on the assignment's question list.

Author new question

This link takes you to the **Author a new question** page, where you can author a new question from scratch and place it in the assignment. Once the question is completed, you can return to the **Assignments/Tests** page with the new question inserted in the assignment.

Edit a selected question

If you have selected a question, use this link to open it for editing in the appropriate authoring editor. Once you have completed your edits on the question, you can return to the **Assignments/ Tests** page with the modified question inserted in the assignment.

Add more questions

Use this link to select new questions to add to the current assignment. It opens the **Choose content** and **Filter** pages to select the additional questions you want to use.

Student View

This option lets you view the selected question as it will appear to the student online.

Printing Assignments

ThomsonNOW provides a wide range of options for creating printed versions of your ThomsonNOW tests and assignments. In addition to specifying layout details, you can print tests from ThomsonNOW content that shuffle problems and regenerate values so that every student gets a unique version of the test every time you print it. These version options increase your ability to easily retest and reinforce learning, and help reduce the potential for casual cheating.

Working with Print Options

You can access your print and print setup options for assignments from the assignment **Format and preview** page. Select the assignment you want to print, and then choose from the following buttons at the bottom of the page:

- ○ Click the **Edit Print Layout** link to select a header and footer, and to access print options.

- ○ Click **Print** to print the selected assignment with your current print settings.

- ○ Click **Save as PDF** to save the selected assignment using your current print settings.

- ○ Click **Change Settings** to choose or change your print options for this assignment. When finished, click **Save** to keep the settings and return to **Format and preview**.

Editing Print Layout

You can quickly select a header and footer to use for your assignment before printing it, or access other print layout options.

From the **Format and preview** page, select the assignment you want to print, and then choose the **Edit Print Layout** link just above the question list. The **Select Header/Footer** pop-up window that appears gives the following options:

Use default header/footer

Select this option and click **Continue** to print the assignment with write-in entry lines for student **Name**, **Class**, and **Date** in the header and page numbers in the footer.

Use my global header/footer

You can create your own "global" header and footer to use on all of your assignments. If you have already created one, and want to use it on this assignment, select this option and click **Continue**. To create your own global header/footer, see "Edit Headers and Footers" on page 111.

Create header/footer for assignment

Select this option to create a header and footer for this assignment only. See "Edit Headers and Footers" on page 111. Once the header and footer are created, click **Continue**.

Edit other print options

Click this link to open the **Printing Options** page to view and edit all aspects of the assignment's print layout, including headers/footers, typeface, and other features.

Setting Print Options

You can customize almost every aspect of your current assignment's print layout and options, and save them for use in other assignments.

Access the **Print Options** page from the **Format and preview** page's **Edit Print Layout** link or **Change settings** button. Make the changes you want and click **Save**, or **Print** to use them immediately.

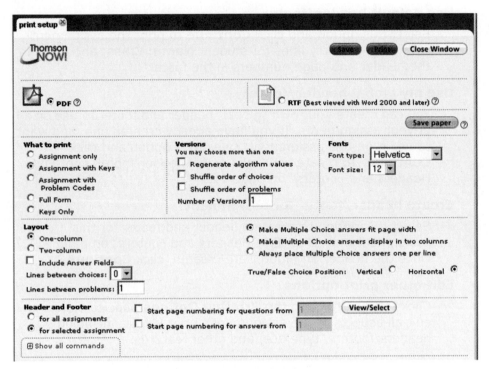

The Print Setup page

Choose output format

ThomsonNOW creates a print file of your assignment, rather than sending it directly to your printer. You can create PDF files or RTF (Rich Text Format) output files. Once these files are created, you print them from outside ThomsonNOW with the appropriate software.

PDF (Portable Document Format)

Select this option to have your assignment saved in the PDF file format. This file format preserves your document's appearance, regardless of how it was created. To view or print PDF files, you need the free Adobe Reader software. If you don't have Adobe Reader software yet, you can get it from Adobe at http://www.adobe.com/products/acrobat/readstep2.html. To edit PDF files, you need Adobe Acrobat® or Acrobat Professional software.

Note: On Macs, you may not be able to open a PDF document created in Windows® just by double-clicking it. Open Adobe Reader and use **File > Open** instead.

RTF (Rich Text Format)

Select this option to have your assignment saved in RTF (Rich Text Format). The RTF file format lets you open and further customize your assignment before printing it. RTF is supported by many word processors, including Microsoft Word (Word 2000 or later recommended) and OpenOffice.org.

Note: If you work with an RTF file in Windows WordPad and then open it in Word, use the "Web View" option to display it properly.

Save Paper

Select this option to print your assignment with the layout options that will use the least paper. This is the ThomsonNOW default layout. See the online Help for the specific settings.

What to print

These settings determine what is included in the print file for your assignment.

Assignment only

Print assignment questions only, not including any answers.

Assignment with Keys

Print assignment questions, and include an answer key on a separate sheet.

Assignment with Problem Codes

Print assignment questions labeled with the source problem's ThomsonNOW name or code (for example, gfia.08.02.4.53) and keys. This helps you identify questions even if they have been shuffled or given regenerated values.

Full Form

This option includes everything: questions, keys, and problem codes.

Keys Only

Print only answer keys.

Versions

These settings let you create distinct test versions from the same set of questions. By shuffling choice sequence, question sequence, and regenerating algorithmic values, you can create as many unique versions of the assignment as you want. These settings increase your ability to easily retest and reinforce learning, and reduce the potential for casual cheating.

You may choose more than one of the following:

Regenerate algorithm values

Regenerates the values of all questions in the assignment with algorithmic values. This option will have no effect on items authored with constant (non-algorithmic) values.

Shuffle order of choices

Within each question, randomly reorders the sequence of answer choices.

Shuffle order of problems

Randomly reorders the sequence of questions in each section of the assignment.

Note: If you select a **Shuffle order** option, you can't choose a custom sort order, and vice versa.

Number of Versions

Enter the number of different versions you want to create and include in the print file or job. The default value is 1 (all identical; no shuffle or regenerate).

Fonts

These settings determine the typeface style and size for the assignment.

Font type

Select the font typeface to use for printing the assignment from the drop-down menu.

Font size

Use the drop-down menu to select the body text font size to use in the printed assignment. A font size of 10 or 12 is typical for printed reading material.

Layout

These options control how questions and answers are arranged on the page.

One-column

Produces a document with all items in a single column.

Two-column

Produces a document printed with two columns. Not available for RTF format output.

Include Answer Fields

Check this box to print short "answer lines" in front of each question: ____1, ____2, etc. The student can use this line to write in the correct answer value.

Lines between choices

Select the number of blank lines (0, 1, 2) between answer choices from the drop-down menu. Default is 0.

Lines between problems

Enter the number of blank lines between problems. Default is 1.

Make Multiple Choice answers fit page width

Arranges Multiple Choice answers to take full advantage of each line's available width.

Make Multiple Choice answers display in two columns

Arranges Multiple Choice answers by alternating them in two columns.

Always place Multiple Choice answers one per line

Prints Multiple Choice answers vertically, each on its own line.

True/False Choice Position

Choose whether True/False answers are arranged horizontally (side by side, same line) or vertically (next line).

Header and footer

These settings determine how the headers and footers you create in the **Edit Headers and Footers** window will be applied.

To access the **Edit Headers and Footers** window, click the **View/Select** button.

For all assignments

Select to edit header and footer settings for all of your assignments.

For selected assignments

Select to change the header or footer for the selected assignment only. Requires that the respective assignment be selected before you open **Print Options**.

Start page numbering for questions from

Sets the beginning page number for questions.

Start page numbering for answers from

Sets the beginning page number for answers.

Print style

Note: The remaining Printing Options are advanced. If necessary, click **Show all commands** to view them.

These settings determine how to translate elements from on-screen assignments to the printed version.

eStyle

(Default) The eStyle format makes the printout resemble an on-screen assignment. For example, the assignment will print with "radio button" circles next to each Multiple Choice or True/False answer for the student to mark.

Standard

The Standard format does not include "on-screen" elements on the printout.

Put grid lines around column Multiple Choice questions

This option applies grid lines around Multiple Choice questions and answers to make the choices and pairings more visually distinct.

Copy selection

These selections give you the option to print out copies for particular courses or students whenever you print the assignment.

Select Course

Check this option to print or quick-view the assignment for a particular course at print time. You'll select the course from a dialog box that appears whenever you print the assignment.

Print Assignment for Selected Students

This option is available if you have selected an assignment prior to opening **Print Options**. Checkmark this option to print or quick-view the assignment for a selected student or group of students at print time. If you also chose **Select Course** (previous setting, above) the students will be limited to those in that course.

When you print the assignment, a dialog box will appear with a drop-down menu to let you select the particular course and students.

Note: If you chose to hide the print-time dialog box, you can enable it again with the **Display Dialog** button in this section.

Sorting options

These options let you put the assignment questions in a specific order, even if that differs from the assignment's current question order.

Note: You won't be able to select a sort option if you selected a "shuffle order" option under **Versions**.

Keep in current order

(Default.) Keeps questions in their original order as built in the assignment.

Sort by problem code

Questions in each section are organized in ascending order by ThomsonNOW problem name (for example, gfia.08.02.4.53, ...54, etc.).

Sort by problem type

Organizes questions in each section by problem type (Multiple Choice, True/False, etc.).

Sort by difficulty

Organizes questions by their difficulty setting, as defined in each problem's **Common Properties**.

Advanced Layout

These options determine specialized effects in the formatting of your printed assignment.

Print formulae in italics

Prints formulae in italics to make them stand out from the plain body text.

Embed all fonts used

This setting "embeds" the font in the print file to ensure the text will be printed in the original font, even if the printing software or printer doesn't have that font installed. Embedding fonts, however, does increase file size.

Show commas in numbers

Shows or removes commas from numbers larger than 999. This is useful for graphs, which are easier to read without commas.

Keep questions and answers on the same page

This setting keeps each question on the same page as its answer, even if much of the adjacent page(s) must be left blank to do it.

Minimize blank space

Lets questions be printed on a different page than their answers. Conserves paper.

Image/graph size

Limit image height or width to 2 inches

Limits printed images to no more than 2 inches by 2 inches. This size is usually adequate for graphs, and can save paper.

Original size

Printouts include images in their original size as authored.

Section breaks

Hidden

Starts each new section of the assignment with no visible section or page break.

New page

Starts each new section of the assignment on a new page.

Paper

Quality

Lets you select a print quality of **Low**, **Medium**, or **High** from the drop-down menu. You normally do not need to use **High** except for complex graphics. Print resolution depends on the capabilities of your computer, software used to print, and printer.

Scale content to

Scales font sizes and graphs on the printed page area by a percentage relative to the right margin. For example, a line of text that reaches the right margin at 100% will reach only halfway at 50%.

Page width

This option allows you to adjust the width of the printed page area. The default is 8.5 inches.

Page height

This option allows you to adjust the height of the printed page area. The default is 11 inches.

Edit Headers and Footers

The header and footer of the assignment are the very top and bottom of each page. You can include such items as page numbers, the date, the assignment title, the student's name, or other information pertinent to the assignment.

You can also specify different information for the first (title) page of the assignment, and the subsequent pages.

When you open the assignment on the **Format and preview** page, you can see the currently selected header/footer. The first and subsequent page headers are displayed just above the question list, while the first and subsequent page footers are displayed just below. Use the "toggle" arrow on the left to expand or contract the display.

Access the **Edit Headers and Footers** window from the **View/Select** button on the **Print Options** page.

Using the Edit Headers and Footers window

This window lets you view the current header/footer, choose a different header/footer, or create a custom header/footer by modifying any of the ready-made templates.

When you access the window, the current header and footer are displayed in the four editing windows. The top two windows are for the first-page header and footer. The bottom two are for the header and footer that appear on the subsequent pages.

Before closing the window, click **Save** to save the current header and footer as part of the print setup.

Header/Footer templates

You have several ready-made header/footer template options available. To choose a template, select it from the **Insert template** drop-down menu at the bottom of the window.

- **Custom Option #1** and **#2** provide basic, workable layouts.

- Use **blank** if you want to start completely from scratch.

- Use **#1 using tables** or **#2 using tables** as your starting point if you want more control over the header/footer spacing and layout. You'll use the ThomsonNOW **HTML Table Editor** if you customize one of these. See "Advanced Header/Footer Layout" on page 113.

Insert Macro

You can customize any of the header and footer templates by typing in text, or selecting header and footer macros from the **Insert Macro** drop-down menu at the bottom of the window.

These macros insert the text you want to appear in a certain spot, such as the page number, assignment name, etc. Try not to insert more macros or text than you really need, or the headers and footers may appear crowded or off-center. Macro options include:

- page number

- current date

- version number

- assignment name

- number of answerable questions

- total possible points

- student name

- student ID

- instructor name

- course name

Advanced Header/Footer Layout

If you want a fine degree of layout control over your assignment headers and footers, you can lay out each header and footer as an inserted table. This provides you better control over element spacing, word wrap, and justification.

- The easiest way to start is to select **#1 as table** or **#2 as table** from the **Header/Footer templates** drop-down menu. You can then view the header and footer layout in the table editor and make adjustments easily.

- To start from scratch, select the **blank** template, and lay it out using the HTML toolbar's **Insert Table** button.

Archiving Courses and Assignments

ThomsonNOW's archiving features let you store folders, courses, sections, and assignments you are not currently using. Items stored in **Archived Materials** are readily available for you to retrieve, delete permanently, or copy into a new folder, course, or section.

The **Archived Materials** page lets you file course materials to retrieve at a later time for reference or for use in future courses. You can archive entire folders, courses, course sections, or individual assignments. There are specific rules, however, about what you can archive and how you retrieve it. You should adhere to the system default selections and prompts to ensure your archived items function correctly when retrieved.

Working with Archived Materials

Use ThomsonNOW's archive features to store folders, courses, sections, and assignments you are not currently using.

Your **Archived Materials** page is automatically organized according to the hierarchical structure of your folders, courses, sections, and assignments. This means that if you archive, for example, a course, any sections and assignments it contains are filed with it. If you want to archive only assignments, you must select and archive them at the assignment level, without selecting their associated sections or courses. If you archive a course section, only section-level assignments, not course-level assignments, will be archived with that section, and so on.

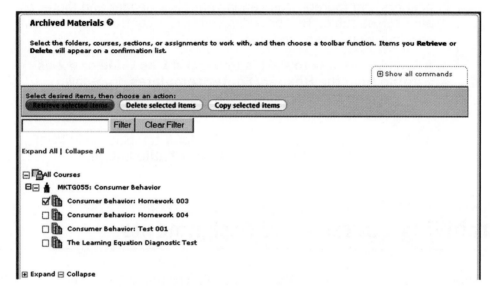

The Archived Materials page

The program follows this same structure when you retrieve assignments. To retrieve an assignment that was archived with its associated section or course, you are prompted to retrieve the relevant section or course as well. To retrieve a section of an archived course, you are also prompted to retrieve its course-level assignments. And if you are a section-level instructor, you must have your course-level instructor retrieve your course-level items for you.

➢ To access Archived Materials from the Assignments/Tests tab

1. On the **Assignments/Tests** page, select the course from which you want to copy archived assignments.

2. Click **Show all commands** to display the archive options.

3. From the **Go to a content source** drop-down menu, select **Archived Materials**.

4. Click the **Go** button, and the **Archived Materials** page opens.

➤ To access Archived Assignments from the Courses tab

1. On the **Courses** tab, click **Show all commands** to display the archive options.

2. Click the **Archived Materials** link to go to the **Archived Materials** page.

Using the Archived Materials page

The **Archived Materials** page shows the organizational hierarchy of your archived items, including icons for folders, courses, sections, and assignments. The archived items themselves display a "file cabinet" icon.

○ Click the **+/-** buttons on each "branch" of the hierarchy "tree" to view (**+**) or hide (**-**) its contents.

○ Use the selection check boxes to select items and item groups for retrieval, copying, or deletion.

○ Some items will "auto-select" based on your selections, showing that the items were archived or organized as a group. Similarly, items with a "dashed" check box have one or more dependent items selected (an assignment in a course, for example).

○ If an item displays a lock icon, you need the necessary system permissions to retrieve, copy, or delete that item.

Archiving your materials

➢ To archive selected folders, courses, and sections

1. On the **Courses** tab, click **Show all commands** to display the archive options.

2. Select the folder, course, or section containing the assignments you wish to archive.

3. From the **Folder Manager** drop-down menu (for folders) OR the **Course Manager** list (for courses), select **Archive** and then click the adjacent **Go** button to archive the selected items.

➢ To archive specific assignments within a course

1. On the **Assignments/Tests** page, first select the appropriate course, and then click **Show all commands** if needed.

2. Select the assignment(s) you want to archive.

3. From the **Assignment Manager** drop-down menu, select **Archive**, and then click the adjacent **Go** button to archive the selected items.

Retrieving items from Archived Materials

Retrieving an item from **Archived Materials** moves it back into the **Courses** or **Assignments/Tests** page where you can actively view and work with it.

➢ To retrieve archived folders, courses, and sections

1. On the **Courses** tab, click **Show all commands** to display the archive options.

2. Click the **Archived Materials** link to go to the **Archived Materials** page.

3. Select the folders, courses, and sections you want to retrieve, and click the **Retrieve selected items** button.

4. In the **Archived Materials - Confirm Item Retrieval** window, review your selections. To retrieve them, click **Retrieve selected items**. To change the selections, click **Change current selections** and change your selections as needed before retrieving them.

➤ To retrieve specific assignments

1. On the **Assignments/Tests** page, select the course for which you want to retrieve assignments, and then click **Go**.

2. Click **Show all commands** to display the archive options.

3. From the **Go to a content source** drop-down menu, select **Archived Materials**, and then click **Go**. The **Archived Materials** page opens.

4. Select the assignment(s) you want to retrieve, and click the **Retrieve selected items** button.

5. In the **Archived Materials - Confirm Item Retrieval** window, review your selections. To retrieve them, click **Retrieve selected items**. To change the selections, click **Change current selections** and change your selections as needed before retrieving them.

Copying items from Archived Materials

You can copy folders, courses, or assignments from **Archived Materials** to the ThomsonNOW clipboard and then paste the items directly into a new folder, course, or section. This shortcut makes it easy to retrieve and update an archived item for a new use, and saves you the work of creating it from scratch each time.

➤ To copy archived folders, courses, and sections

1. On the **Courses** page, click **Show all commands** to display the archive options.

2. Click the **Archived Materials** link to open the **Archived Materials** page.

3. Select the folders, courses, and sections you want to copy, and click the **Copy selected items** button.

4. Click the **Go to courses** link on the right-hand side of the page.

5. On the **Courses** page, select the appropriate course into which you want to copy the archived items, and click **Go**.

6. Click **Paste from clipboard** (in **Show all commands**) to paste the copied items from the ThomsonNOW clipboard into the selected course or section.

➤ To copy specific assignments

1. On the **Assignments/Tests** tab, select the course from which you want to copy archived assignments, and click **Go**.

2. Click **Show all commands** to display the archive options.

3. From the **Go to a content source** drop-down menu, select **Archived Materials**, and then click the **Go** button.

4. On the **Archived Materials** page, select the assignments you want to copy, and click the **Copy selected items** button.

Note: If you simply want to return the archived assignments to the original course, use **Retrieve selected items** instead.

---

5. Click the **Assignments/Tests** tab.

6. On the **Assignments/Tests** page, open the appropriate course or section into which you want to paste the copied assignments, and click **Show all commands**.

7. Click **Paste from clipboard** to paste the copied assignments from the ThomsonNOW clipboard into the selected course or section.

Deleting archived items

You can delete items permanently from your archive if you feel you need to reduce clutter or save disk space. Keep in mind that deleted items are gone for good. If there is any chance you may need to access that assignment, course, or student grade again, it's best to just archive it and keep it there.

➢ To delete archived folders, courses, and sections

1. On the **Courses** tab, click **Show all commands** to display the archive options.

2. Click the **Archived Materials** link to go to the **Archived Materials** page.

3. Select the folders, courses, and sections you want to delete, and click the **Delete selected items** button.

4. In the **Confirm Item Deletion** window, review your selections. Once you have confirmed that you do indeed wish to permanently delete these items, click **Delete selected items**. To change the selections, click **Change current selections** and change your selections as needed before deleting.

Caution: We strongly suggest you adhere to the system default selections and prompts when deleting items. For example, say you archive an entire course but later delete some of its assignments. If you later retrieve that course, its **Gradebook** records will reflect only the remaining assignments and won't match other course records you might have.

➢ To delete specific archived assignments

1. On the **Assignments/Tests** tab, select the course from which you wish to delete archived assignments, and click **Go**.

2. Click **Show all commands** to display the archive options.

3. From the **Go to a content source** drop-down menu, select **Archived Materials**, and click the **Go** button.

4. On the **Archived Materials** page, select the assignments you want to delete, and click the **Delete selected items** button.

5. In the **Confirm Item Deletion** window, review your selections. Once you have confirmed that you do indeed wish to permanently delete these items, click **Delete selected items**. To change the selections, click **Change current selections** and change your selections as needed before deleting.

Working with Master Files

A **Master File** is a by-product of creating an assignment. It is essentially just the set of questions you've selected from your source materials: a generic "unassigned assignment" so to speak. The **Master File** is a convenient source of new and future assignments.

Note: In previous versions of ThomsonNOW (i.e., iLrn), **Master Files** were known as "assessments." Many of the features formerly on the **Manage Assessments** page are now integrated into the Create Assignment process.

The Master Files Page

The **Master Files** page lets you accumulate a personal store of assessment material and question banks to be mixed and matched according to your course needs. Use the **Master Files** page to manage, modify, and assign the **Master Files** you build, or publish them as **WebQuizzes** or online tutorials.

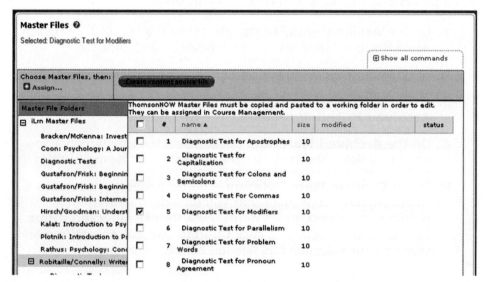

Master Files page

➤ To access the Master Files page

1. On the **Assignments/Tests** page, choose the appropriate course from the drop-down menu, and then click the adjacent **Go** button.

2. If necessary, click **Show all commands** to show advanced commands.

3. From the **Go to a content source** drop-down menu, select **Master Files**, and click **Go**.

➤ Managing the Master Files list

The **Master File** page is your storehouse for assignment content you use repeatedly. Its features help you find the **Master File** you want quickly.

Master File Folders

You will start with a **My Master Files** folder to store the assignments you create. If you wish, you can click its **Create Subfolder** icon to create new subfolders for organizing and storing your **Master Files**. These subfolders can be deleted or renamed as needed.

ThomsonNOW Assessments Folder

Depending on your school and registered ThomsonNOW content, you may also have a **ThomsonNOW Master Files** folder. This folder contains pre-built assignment forms associated with your book. These forms can include sample homework, test banks, diagnostic tests, and Practice State Proficiency exams.

You can assign a form assignment "as is" from **Assignments/ Tests > Create Assignment > Choose from Pre-built Assignments**. If you prefer to edit or customize it first, you can open the **ThomsonNOW Master Files** folder here, select the **Master File** you want, then copy and paste it into one of your working folders under **My Master Files**. You can then edit the problems and properties to customize it before assigning it to a course.

Sort the Master Files list

Simply click the column headings for **Master File** name, size (in questions) and last-modified date to sort them in ascending order, or again to reverse.

Search for a Master File

Enter a key term from the **Master File** name or content, and then click **Find Master File**.

Show all commands

Click this link to reveal the clipboard functions (**Cut**, **Copy**, **Delete**, **Paste**), the Printing and Viewing options, as well as the **Master File Import**, **Export**, and **Analyze** options. To conceal these commands again, click **Hide these commands**.

➤ Assigning a Master File

You can create an assignment from a **Master File** by selecting assignment options for it and assigning it to a class. The new assignment will then be accessible from the **Assignments/Tests** page. The **Master File** remains available for creating additional assignments.

1. On the **Master File** page, select the **Master File** you want to assign, and then click the **Assign...** link.

2. The **Modify assignment options** page will open to let you determine the assignment's options, print layout, and behavior. See "Choosing Assignment Options" on page 75 and "Printing Assignments" on page 102 for how to set assignment and print options.

➤ Renaming a Master File

You can change the name of a **Master File** to account for a change in its content or purpose. (If you want to retain a copy of the **Master File** with its original name, copy the **Master File** first, paste it, and then rename the copy.)

1. On the **Master File** page, select the **Master File** you want to rename, and then click the **Rename** link.

2. On the **Rename Master File** page, type the new name for the **Master File** into the text field, and click the **Rename** button.

   The **Master File** now appears on the **Master File** page with this new name.

➢ Editing a Master File

You can edit a **Master File** to rename it, add new items, remove items, or change the item order. You can also change the internal authoring for questions (for advanced users only).

1. On the **Master File** page, click on the name of the **Master File** you want to edit (or select the file and then click the **Edit this Master File** link).

2. The **Format and preview** page will open to let you reorder or reselect the questions. See "Format and preview the assignment" on page 70 for details.

3. After making the formatting changes you want, you can **Save** the **Master File**, as well as complete the process of assigning it to a class if you want.

Additional Master Files Commands

To see these additional **Master Files** page commands, click **Show all commands**. To conceal them, click **Hide all commands**.

Choose Master Files, then . . .

Print Options

Access your print setup options to define headers, footers, problem layout, typeface, and other aspects of the printed assignment.

Print

Use this link to print the **Master File** using your current print options.

View selected Master File

Use this link to open the selected **Master File** for editing in the **Format and preview** page, where you can rename the file, and reorder and change the questions.

Quick view

Use this link to preview the **Master File** rendered in HTML (web page format). This view gives you an approximate idea of how the assignment will appear when printed out or viewed online.

➤ Creating a WebQuiz

You can easily post your **Master File** as a **WebQuiz** to a web address where it can be accessed by anyone using any web browser, with or without ThomsonNOW. Users go to the appropriate URL, or web address as generated by ThomsonNOW, to take the **WebQuiz**. The **WebQuiz** score is then reported to you via e-mail.

You have the additional option of designating the **WebQuiz** as an External assignment. The difference is as follows:

- ○ When a student takes a stand-alone **WebQuiz**, their results are reported to you via automatic e-mail.

- ○ When a student takes a **WebQuiz** that has been set up as an External assignment, the assignment can still be accessed outside of ThomsonNOW. However, the student's results flow directly into your ThomsonNOW **Gradebook**.

WebQuizzes offer an important tool for online assessment. You can post an accessible, customized **WebQuiz** from any ThomsonNOW **Master File** to a complete class in a matter of minutes.

1. From the **Master Files** page, click **Show all commands** if you have not already done so.

2. Select the **Master File** you want to post on the web.

3. From the **Master File Manager** drop-down menu, select **Publish as a WebQuiz** and click the adjacent **Go** button.

4. On the **WebQuiz Properties** page, select **Publish as a WebQuiz**, and then click **Save My Changes**. ThomsonNOW will display the generated URL (web address) for your **WebQuiz**.

5. At this point, the **WebQuiz** is complete. Click the **Return to Master Files** link to exit.

   You may copy and paste the URL into an e-mail or text document to distribute to your students. To access the **WebQuiz** again, find it on your **Assignments/Tests** tab, marked with the blue clock status icon.

   To see how to set up the **WebQuiz** as an External assignment (so that the results flow into your **Gradebook**), see "Creating an External Assignment" on page 96.

➤ Importing a Master File

Choose **Import** to import ThomsonNOW **Master Files**, test banks, and other assignment source files. Any valid BCA format file saved using the ThomsonNOW **Export as XML** option can be imported into your system. If these files have been exported with all necessary linked content, you can import and use them without access to the parent test bank.

1. From the **Master Files Manager** drop-down menu (click **Show all commands** if necessary), select **Import** and click the adjacent **Go** button.

2. Click the **Browse** button and navigate through the folders on your system to locate the file(s) you want to import.

Note: If you are working with a file containing several **Master Files** (such as a compressed TGZ or ZIP file), you should uncompress the file and import the individual **Master Files** separately.

---

3. If you have several files to import, you can use the **Add more files** link to add more files to the list, *or* **Remove this file** to remove files from the list.

4. Click the **Import** button to import the selected files.

Once the file has been imported, it will be available on the **Master Files** page for you to view, edit, or assign.

Exporting Master Files in XML format

You can export the **Master Files** you create in ThomsonNOW to many different formats. These formats include ThomsonNOW's native XML format, as well as WebCT®, Blackboard®, or ExamView®, among others. This lets you share your ThomsonNOW **Master Files** with colleagues, or use them in other software packages.

Export to other ThomsonNOW users

Select **Export as XML**. This is ThomsonNOW's native format and ensures full support for all problem types. The XML option lets you export a **Master File** from the ThomsonNOW database as an XML file that can be loaded (imported) onto any ThomsonNOW server. This means you can move or share the test you created on your personal (local) server to your school's LAN or to your account on the ThomsonNOW server at http://www.ilrn.com.

Note: You can export **Master Files** individually to XML in the BCA format. You can also export multiple files as a single compressed ZIP file, allowing them to be stored or e-mailed more conveniently.

Include ThomsonNOW problem content

When you build an assignment from ThomsonNOW content, you are creating a set of dynamic XML links to the items in your ThomsonNOW books and forms. If you are exporting a **Master File** to someone who may not have access to the same ThomsonNOW books you used to build the **Master File**, you can select **Include ThomsonNOW problem content**. Including the content in the export file will result in a larger file, but ensures that the assignment will work correctly whether or not the user has access to the same book(s).

Note: Including problem content for ThomsonNOW problems "de-links" the exported problems from the source book. This means that if the problems are subsequently updated in the ThomsonNOW source book, the exported, de-linked problems will NOT be dynamically updated. On the other hand, self-authored questions and ThomsonNOW book problems that you have copied and modified are already "de-linked," and will always include problem content when exported.

➤ To export Master Files as XML

1. On the **Master Files** page (click **Show all commands** if necessary), select the file(s) you want to export.

   Note: (If you select multiple files, they will be exported in a single compressed ZIP format file).

   ---

2. From the **Master File Manager** drop-down menu, select **Export** and click the adjacent **Go** button.

3. Click **Include ThomsonNOW problem content** if you want to ensure that the assignment will work correctly whether or not the user has access to the same book(s).

4. Click **Export as XML**.

5. Click **Save**, confirm the file name and location, and then click **Save** again to complete the export.

➢ Exporting Master Files to other software

You can export ThomsonNOW **Master Files** to several other educational software packages and classroom response systems, including WebCT, Blackboard, and TurningPoint®.

Note: ThomsonNOW supports a large number of problem types that are not available in or supported by other software packages. As a result, the export format you select determines the type of questions you can export from ThomsonNOW.

---

1. On the **Master Files** page (click **Show all commands** if necessary), select the file you want to export.

   Note: Files exported to non-ThomsonNOW software must be exported one file at a time.

   ---

2. From the **Master File Manager** drop-down menu, select **Export** and click the adjacent **Go** button.

3. Click the link for the desired export format.

4. Follow the on-screen instructions to finish the export.

You will be able to review any problem types in your **Master File** that are not supported in the selected export format. Only the supported problem types will be exported. Refer to the ThomsonNOW online Help for details and specific examples.

COURSE MATERIALS

The **Course Materials** tab displays the Thomson textbooks and courseware with online materials that you can access through ThomsonNOW.

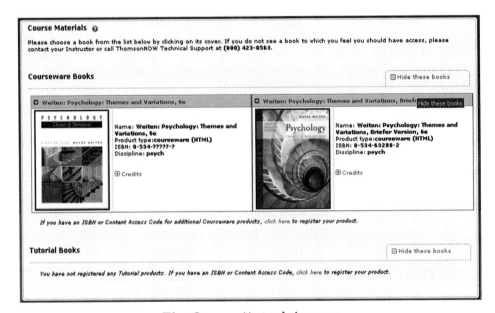

The Course Materials page

To see your book on this page, you must have successfully registered the book using its **Content Access Code**. You can register your book during your initial ThomsonNOW registration or by using the link on the **Course Materials** page.

Once you have registered the book, simply click on the picture of your book's cover on the **Course Materials** page to access any of its online materials for your online reading or practice.

Note: You may see some of the same material in your course assignments that you do in **Course Materials**, but there are key differences:

○ Course assignments taken from the **Assignments** page are graded ThomsonNOW coursework.

○ Work completed in the **Course Materials** area is typically ungraded practice or self-study.

Once the book is registered, the student can access all of its available online contents directly from this page. Depending on the book, the student may be able to do the following:

○ **Reading**. Some or all of the textbook reading matter will be available for access and reading online.

○ **Diagnostics**. Some books offer online diagnostic pretests that assess your students' initial grasp of the subject content and highlight areas where students need more work.

○ **Tutorials**. Most books provide tutorial supplements that expand on the subject matter with practice problems, example walkthroughs, and interactive demonstrations or simulations.

○ **Exercises and Practice Tests**. Students may be able to take practice homework and tests online to help reinforce learning and prepare for class assignments and tests.

COMMUNICATION

You can use the features on the **Communication** tab to post messages to your students or other instructors, and to organize and monitor online discussion groups for your courses. For example, you can maintain ongoing "bulletin board" dialogs with your students on particular topic threads, view system messages and alerts, or establish online office hours during which you are available to answer questions from students.

Discussions

This area displays all of the current discussion groups, topics, and actions available to you.

Communication Tools

These links let you access discussion links for a specific course, or contact ThomsonNOW Technical Support.

Messages & Alerts

These links will display messages of interest to all ThomsonNOW users at your school, such as new-feature notices and scheduled maintenance releases.

Working with Discussion Groups

Discussion groups are a useful means for conducting communications with the students in your courses. You typically will have at least one discussion group for each course, but you may have more.

To create a discussion group, first go to the **Communication** tab.

Creating a Discussion Group

Select the course in which you want to create the discussion group, and then click the **Create Discussion Group** button. Enter the topic title or name of the discussion group you want to create, and then click the **Submit** link. The new group will appear on your **Discussions** list.

As new discussion groups are added to your list, you will see that you can sort the list by **Course**, **Topic**, number of **Replies**, and **Last Modified** by clicking on the column headers. The **Actions** column provides links for specific things you can do within the group.

Creating a Discussion Topic

To start a new topic for your discussion group, first click the **See Discussion** link in the **Actions** column. Click the **Start a New Topic** button, enter a title for the topic, and then click the **Submit** link.

As new discussions are added to your list, you will see that you can sort the list by **Topic**, **Replies**, **Submitted by**, and **Last Modified** by simply clicking on the column headers. The **Actions** column provides links for specific things you can do within the group.

Creating a Discussion Message

To add a new message to a discussion, first select the discussion group and topic. Click **Add a New Message**, enter the text for your message or reply using the WYSIWYG (What You See Is What You Get) editor tools, and then click the **Submit** link.

Once your message is posted, you can edit, delete it, or reply to it.

Note: Students can reply to messages posted by others but cannot edit or delete them. Only instructors can edit or delete messages posted by others in their group.

To attach a file to your message (for example, a JPG image or a PDF document), click **Attach**, browse to the file on your computer, and select it.

To remove an attached file, select its check box under **Detach**, and click **Submit**.

AUTHORING IN THOMSONNOW

Electronic assignments and test banks offer thousands of ready-made questions that can be continually refreshed with automatic shuffling and (for math problems) algorithmic regeneration. These robust features enable you to build assignments that remain fresh indefinitely. As an added benefit, Authoring features allow you to create your own Self-Authored Questions, or copy and modify any of the items in your question banks.

Using ThomsonNOW's Authoring features, you can:

○ Create personal folders to contain questions

○ Modify existing questions

○ Edit questions for specific assignments

○ Create new questions

The following pages introduce the features of the **Self-Authored Questions** page and the ThomsonNOW Problem Editors. For details on how to use the editors to create or modify questions, refer to the ThomsonNOW Help for Authoring.

Self-Authored Questions

You can create new questions and store edited questions for future assignments using features on the **Self-Authored Questions** page. You can cut or copy problems from any assignment and store them here for reuse, with or without modification. You can also organize your questions in your **Self-Authored Questions** folder(s).

You have two ways to open the **Self-Authored Questions** page.

○ From your **Home** Page, click the **Author New Questions** quick link (you can enable/disable this link from your **Home** page **Preferences**), or

○ From **Assignments**, click **Show all commands**. Then from the **Go to a content source** drop-down menu, select **Self-Authored Questions** and click **Go**.

Working with Self-Authored Questions Folders

On the left side of the **Self-Authored Questions** page, you can create **Self-Authored Questions** subfolders to organize your questions by type, difficulty, course, or any other categories you want.

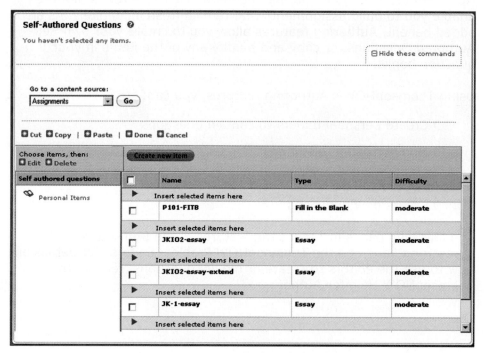

The Self-Authored Questions page

➢ To create a folder

On the **Self-Authored Questions** page, you can create and organize the subfolders in your **Self-Authored Questions** area as you wish.

1. Click the **Create Sub-folder** icon next to the **Self-Authored Questions** folder.

2. Click the adjacent **Rename** icon.

3. Replace the default folder name by typing in the new name, and then click the adjacent **Save** icon.

➤ To rename a folder

Once you've created a **Self-Authored Questions** subfolder, you can go back at any time and change its name.

1. Select the folder you want to rename, and click adjacent **Rename** icon.

2. In the text box that appears, replace the displayed folder name by typing in the new name, and then click the adjacent **Save** icon.

➤ To delete a folder

If necessary, you can delete a **Self-Authored Questions** subfolder and all of the questions and other subfolders it contains. While this deletes the original questions stored in the folder, it does not delete or otherwise affect any copies of these questions that have been added to an assignment previously.

1. Select the subfolder you want to delete.

2. Click the adjacent **Delete** icon.

3. A dialog box will appear to confirm the action. To proceed with the deletion, click **OK**.

Modifying Assignment Items

With ThomsonNOW, you can author your own questions from scratch, reuse or modify existing questions you've already created, or edit questions pulled straight from your available question banks (e.g., test bank).

In most cases, your best approach is to create new questions or save edited questions directly in the **Self-Authored Questions** folder on your **Self-Authored Questions** page. This allows you to easily access the stored question to add it to any of your assignments.

When you create or edit a question within a particular assignment, your new or modified question will be saved in that assignment only. You always have the option, however, of copying and saving an assignment question to **Self-Authored Questions** as well.

Editing an Assignment Item

You can customize a question after it has been added to an assignment. It is strongly recommended, however, that you finish editing your questions *before* adding them to an assignment, or at least before making the assignment available to students. If you edit questions in an active assignment, you may create grading inconsistencies between those students who take the assignment before your changes, and those who take it after.

➢ To edit a question in an assignment

1. On your **Assignments/Tests** tab, select the course containing the assignment you want to edit, and click **Go**.

2. Click the name of the assignment.

3. On the **View/Edit Assignment** page, click **Format and Preview assignment content**.

4. In **Format and preview**, click **Show all commands**.

5. Select the question you want to edit, and then click **Edit a selected question.** The appropriate Problem Editor will open. See "Problem Editors" on page 139 for an overview. See the ThomsonNOW Help on Authoring for more details on using the Problem Editors.

6. Edit the problem as you wish. Click **Save** to save it, and then click **Done** to return to the **Format and preview** page.

The problem will be changed in the current assignment. To use the modified problem elsewhere, be sure to copy it to **Self-Authored Questions**.

Cutting, Copying, and Pasting Assignment Items

Questions you cut or copy from an assignment are placed on the ThomsonNOW clipboard. From the clipboard, you can paste the questions into your **Self-Authored Questions** folders or into other assignments.

➤ To cut or copy items from an assignment

1. On your **Assignments/Tests** tab, select the course that contains the assignment with the question(s) you want, and click **Go**.

2. Click the name of the assignment.

3. On the **View/Edit Assignment** page, click **Format and Preview assignment content**.

4. In **Format and preview**, click **Show all commands**.

5. Select a question you want to take from the assignment, and then click **Cut** or **Copy** to place the question on the ThomsonNOW clipboard.

Note: A cut item will not be removed from the current assignment until you paste it elsewhere.

---

6. Select and cut/copy any additional questions you want to place on the clipboard.

Note: Copied items can be pasted into more than one assignment or folder. They remain on the clipboard until you delete them.

Cut items are automatically deleted from the clipboard when you paste them.

➤ To paste questions into Self-Authored Questions

By saving your new or modified questions in your **Self-Authored Questions** folder(s), you can easily access them to add to any of your assignments.

1. With one or more questions cut or copied to your ThomsonNOW clipboard, go to your **Self-Authored Questions** page.

2. Choose or create a folder in which to store the questions on the clipboard.

3. Click **Paste**. The ThomsonNOW clipboard window opens.

4. Select the check box for each item you want to paste in this current folder; clear the check boxes for items you don't want to paste here.

5. To retain copied items in the clipboard so you can paste them in more than one place, clear the check box for the **Remove copied items from clipboard when pasted?** option. Otherwise, select the check box.

Note: When you paste an item that was cut from an assignment, it is automatically deleted from the assignment and the clipboard.

---

6. Click **Paste**.

The items will be pasted into the selected **Self-Authored Questions** folder. From there, you will be able to edit the problems, copy them to existing assignments, or select them when creating a new assignment.

➤ To paste questions into an assignment

1. With cut or copied questions in the clipboard, go to your **Assignments/Tests** tab, select the course with the assignment you want to edit, and click **Go**.

2. Click the name of the assignment into which you want to paste the questions.

3. On the **View/Edit Assignment** page, click **Format and Preview assignment content**.

4. In **Format and preview**, click **Show all commands**.

5. In the assignment, select the insertion location for the question that should come just before the new, inserted question, and click **Paste**. The ThomsonNOW clipboard opens in a separate window.

6. Select the check box for each item you want to paste in this current folder; clear the check boxes for items you don't want to paste here.

7. To retain copied items in the clipboard so you can paste them in more than one place, clear the check box for the **Remove copied items from clipboard when pasted?** option. Otherwise, select the check box.

> **Note:** When you paste an item that was cut from an assignment, it is automatically deleted from the assignment and the clipboard.

---

8. Click **Paste** to insert the selected items and renumber the problems below it.

Problem Editors

ThomsonNOW includes two powerful tools to help you author your own questions or modify copies of test bank questions:

○ The Standard Problem Editor is used to create or edit basic questions.

○ The Advanced Problem Editor is used for question types of greater complexity.

Both editors can be used to create new questions or to change an existing question's wording, values, hints, correct answer(s), and possible score. Each editor flags errors in your questions with a built-in analyzer, and provides online Help links for its various functions

Within Authoring, ThomsonNOW creates copies of the original questions in your **Self-Authored Questions** folder(s) for you to edit. You do not have to worry about "breaking" the electronic content of your ThomsonNOW books or test banks, because the original questions are "de-linked"; you can't harm them. What's more, book updates won't overwrite or otherwise affect your copies of the questions.

A brief introduction to the two Problem Editors follows. For details on how to use these editors, and for tutorials on how to build the basic problem types, please refer to the ThomsonNOW Help for Authoring.

The Standard Problem Editor

The Standard Problem Editor lets you enter questions and answers in a single page, using our familiar HTML editor interface for editing and formatting text in the question, answer, hints, and feedback areas.

Use the Standard Problem Editor to create or edit ThomsonNOW's most popular problem types:

- ○ Essay

- ○ FITB (Fill in the Blank)

- ○ Multiple Choice

- ○ Matching

- ○ Submission

- ○ True/False

- ○ Free-Response Math

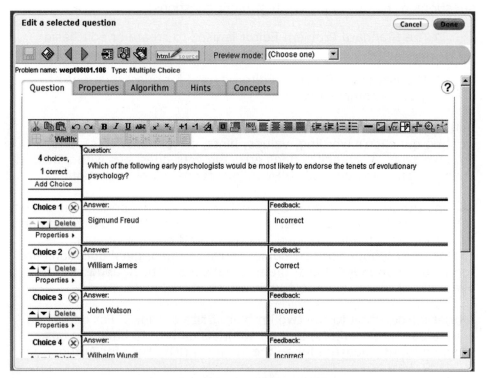

The Standard Problem Editor

The Advanced Problem Editor

The Advanced Problem Editor offers editing capabilities for a wider range of more complex problem types.

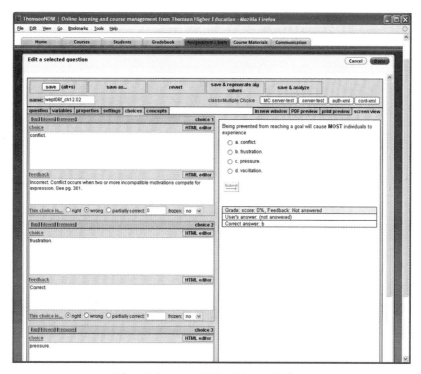

The Advanced Problem Editor

In the Advanced Problem Editor, the source code view is the default (although you can still use the HTML view to edit portions of the questions). A variety of editor panes lets you specify the correct answers, edit algorithms, and change other settings.

Note: The Standard Problem Editor opens by default when you open a standard problem type for editing in **Assignments/Tests** or create a new one in **Self-Authored Questions**. If you prefer to use the Advanced Problem Editor only, click **Preferences** at the top of the page and select **Use the advanced problem editor for authoring all problem types.** Then click **Save these changes**.

See the ThomsonNOW online Help for details and examples of how to use the Problem Editors, or contact Technical Support at supportteam@ilrn-support.com.

WebCT and Blackboard

If you use either **WebCT®** or **Blackboard®** as your online teaching platform, you can use ThomsonNOW's assignment and grade management features when your institution purchases a Thomson published course cartridge.

By using a Thomson content cartridge and ePack, you are automatically signed in to ThomsonNOW when you sign in to either WebCT or Blackboard (known as "single sign-on"). This seamless integration with ThomsonNOW provides a consolidated student roster and **Gradebook** in both applications.

Course cartridge

A software bundle that comes ready to use with all the course content you need. Depending on the particular title bundle, your course cartridge may contain media, book content, and quizzes.

ePack

A software plug-in that allows communication between your institution's server and the WebCT/Blackboard servers.

Note: WebCT calls this ePack a Powerlink, while Blackboard calls it a Building Block.

Generally, your system administrator configures the WebCT or Blackboard ePack installation for you. If your institution has given you a blank course shell and requested you to upload your course's ePack, see the directions available at http://www.webct.com/quickstart/viewpage?name=quickstart_e-pack_quickstart_upload for more help for WebCT. For help with Blackboard installation, go to their customer support website at http://support.blackboard.com/b3/index.aspx.

If you should need information or training on designing your online courses, please contact your Thomson sales representative for either product.

Note: Check to be sure your system meets the ThomsonNOW System Requirements before you start setting up your courses and assignments.

Features

ThomsonNOW offers its powerful features for creating assignments and managing grades for Blackboard and WebCT users:

Grading

The ThomsonNOW **Gradebook** integrates seamlessly with the grading functions in both WebCT and Blackboard. From the main **Grades** page, you can review and edit student grades in several ways. You can also review and edit individual assignment details online, produce a range of grade reports, and view assignments and grades from the student's view.

Assignment Creation

You can easily create activities in ThomsonNOW by using the assignment builder. This option creates a live online or printed assignment from your course content. You can also edit a finished assignment to adapt it quickly for new uses.

Assignment Management

Once you have created your assignments, you can assign them using the default properties, reconfigure them by editing their properties, or even add new or additional items.

Authoring Questions

ThomsonNOW allows you to author your own questions in a wide variety of popular and easy-to-use question formats, including Multiple Choice, True/False, Essay, and Fill in the Blank. You can then include these questions in your assignments along with questions drawn from your ThomsonNOW books.

Note: For details on these procedures, refer to your ThomsonNOW online Help.

TECHNICAL SUPPORT

If you have trouble signing in, or registering your classes or materials, you can contact Thomson Technical Support by telephone, via the online Technical Support form in ThomsonNOW, or by e-mail.

E-mail

supportteam@ilrn-support.com
(usually responds within 48 hours)

Technical Support form

Click the **Technical Support** link at the bottom of the ThomsonNOW Welcome page at http://www.ilrn.com.

Phone

1-888-281-2990

Monday–Friday, 7:00 a.m. to 6:00 p.m. Pacific time

When contacting Technical Support, please provide the following information:

○ First and last name

○ School (including campus)

○ Operating system

○ Browser

○ Content Access Code or textbook ISBN

INDEX

Q

R

S